Social Studies Alive!®
My Community

Chief Executive Officer: Bert Bower

Chief Operating Officer: Amy Larson

Director of Product Development: Liz Russell

Managing Editor: Laura Alavosus

Editorial Project Manager: Lara Fox

Project Editor: Nancy O'Leary

Editorial Associates: Anna Embree and Sarah Sudano

Production Manager: Lynn Sanchez

Design Manager: Jeff Kelly

Graphic Designer: JoAnn Kolonick

Photo Edit Manager: Margee Robinson

Photo Editor: Elaine Soares

Art Editor: Eric Houts

Audio Manager: Katy Haun

TCi™ Teachers' Curriculum Institute
PO Box 50996
Palo Alto, CA 94303

Customer Service: 800-497-6138
www.teachtci.com

ISBN 978-1-58371-801-8

2 3 4 5 6 7 8 9 10 -WC- 15 14 13 12 11 10 09

Program Director
Bert Bower

Program Consultant
Vicki LaBoskey, Ph.D., Professor of Education, Mills College, Oakland, California

Student Edition Writers
Laura M. Alavosus
Susan Buckley
Wendy Frey

Curriculum Developer
Joyce Bartky

Reading Specialist
Barbara Schubert, Ph.D., Reading Specialist, Saint Mary's College, Moraga, California

Teacher Consultants
Jill Bartky, Teacher, Sharp Park Elementary School, Pacifica, California

Debra Elsen, Teacher, Manchester Elementary, Manchester, Maryland

Gina Frazzini, Literary Coach, Gatzert Elementary, Seattle, Washington

Mitch Pascal, Social Studies Specialist, Arlington County Schools, Arlington, Virginia

Becky Suthers, Retired Teacher, Stephen F. Austin Elementary, Weatherford, Texas

Beth Yankee, Teacher, The Woodward School for Technology and Research, Kalamazoo, Michigan

Literature Consultant
Regina M. Rees, Ph.D., Assistant Professor, Beeghly College of Education, Youngstown State University, Youngstown, Ohio

Music Specialist
Beth Yankee, Teacher, The Woodward School for Technology and Research, Kalamazoo, Michigan

Maps
Mapping Specialists, Ltd. Madison, Wisconsin

Contents

Chapter 1

What Is a Community? 3

Learn what makes a place a community. Read about what people do in a community.

Reading Further: One Community's History

Chapter 2

How Are Communities Different? 13

Learn about three kinds of communities. Read about life in the city. Read about life in the country.

Reading Further: Instant Suburbs

Chapter 3

How Do We Use Maps? 25

Learn about maps. Read about the parts of a map. Discover how to read a map.

Reading Further: Mapping a Trip

Chapter 4

What Is Geography? 37

Learn about the geography of different communities. Discover the features of geography on a map.

Reading Further: Riding for Climate

Chapter 5

How Do People Use Our Environment? 49

Learn about nature and different environments. Discover how people use and sometimes hurt their environment.

Reading Further: Using Plants in New Ways

Chapter 6

How Are Goods Made and Brought to Us? 63

Read about what is grown on farms and made in factories. Learn how goods are brought to stores for people to buy.

Reading Further: Food from the Desert

Chapter 7

Who Provides Services in a Community? **77**

Learn what service jobs are. Read about people who do these jobs in a community.

Reading Further: Caring for Central Park

Chapter 8

How Can I Be a Good Shopper? **87**

Learn about needs and wants. Discover ways to be a good shopper.

Reading Further: Shopping for School

Chapter 9

How Do Communities Change? **97**

Read about how a city can change over time. Learn how people can make their city a better place to live.

Reading Further: Los Angeles Grows

Chapter 10

How Did One Community Change? 107

Read about the city of San Francisco. Lean how it changed from a small town to a big city.

Reading Further: Family Stories

Chapter 11

How Can One Person Make a Difference in a Community? . . 119

Read about four people from the past. Discover how they helped their communities.

Reading Further: Homework Help

Chapter 12

How Do Leaders Help Their Communities? 129

Learn how communities choose leaders. Read about the important things leaders do for their communities.

Reading Further: Leaders Vote for the Dogs

Chapter 13

**What Does a Good
Citizen Do?** **139**

Read about good citizens. Learn what
you can do to be a good citizen.

Reading Further: Good Citizen Lincoln

Chapter 14

**What Do Communities
Share?** **149**

Read about things that communities
share with each other. Learn why it is
important for communities to help each
other.

Reading Further: Happy Birthday, USA!

**Landmarks of Citizenship: Special
Days, Special Places** **161**

Atlas **174**

Glossary **182**

Credits **194**

Maps

Washington, D.C. Map **26**

Farm Map **27**

Downtown Centerville **28**

Streets of Centerville **29**

The National Mall **34**

Physical Map of the United States **42**

Ride for Climate USA, 2007 .... **46**

Cotton Growing in the South, 1850 ... **59**

The All American Canal **72**

Los Angeles Past and Present **104**

The United States of America **150**

What Is a Community?

In this chapter, you will learn what a **community** is. It is a place where people live, work, and play. A community is also a place where people solve problems together.

1.1 A Place to Live

A community is a place where people live.
Some people live in houses. Some people
live in apartments. Some people live in
mobile homes. Does everyone have a home
to live in?

1.2 A Place to Work

A community is a place where people work. Some people work in offices. Some people work in factories. Others work in stores and restaurants. Some people work indoors. Some people work outdoors. Where do people work in your community?

1.3 A Place to Play

A community is a place where people play. People like to have fun. Many people have fun at playgrounds. Some people like to go to movies. Others have fun at museums. Where do you have fun in your community?

1.4 A Place to Solve Problems

A community is a place where people solve problems together.

Some people go to city hall to solve problems. Some meet at a school. Some meet at a community center.

Where do people you know go to solve problems? Is there more than one place?

CITY HALL

Summary

A community is a place where people live, work, and play. It is also a place where people solve problems together.

One Community's History

Every community has a history. History is the story of what happened in the past. How is one family part of its community's past?

Christina and Richard Anderson love Marshall, Texas. They live in a very old house there. Richard's great-great uncle built the house in 1845. Richard's family has lived in Marshall for more than 150 years! They are part of the community's history.

This is the Andersons' home.

Richard was born in Marshall. He grew up there. He went to school in the town and played in its parks. When Richard bought his house, he wanted to find out more about Marshall's past.

Richard looked at old photographs. He found old pictures of his house. He found letters that his great-great uncle wrote. He found some things that were in the house long ago. All of these helped Richard learn about Marshall and his house long ago.

These things helped Richard learn about the past.

Richard is a judge. He is proud of the old courthouse.

Christina learned about Marshall's history, too. She talked to people. She read old news articles. She found photographs at the library.

Christina learned that Marshall was formed in 1841. Someone gave land for a courthouse, a church, and a school.

Over time, Marshall grew. People came to work on the railroad. They came to buy and sell cotton. Then they built homes in the town.

When the courthouse was 100 years old, Marshall celebrated. Christina helped give a birthday party for the courthouse.

Richard and Christina help Marshall take care of its past. Richard raises money for Wiley College. It is one of the oldest African American colleges in the country.

Christina planned a garden. It will honor Lady Bird Johnson. Lady Bird was the wife of President Lyndon Johnson. Lady Bird went to high school in Marshall when she was young.

The Andersons are excited about Marshall's future, too. "There is so much good we have built on. And there is so much good yet to be done," Christina said.

Christina planned a garden to celebrate Lady Bird Johnson's life.

How Are Communities Different?

Communities come in different sizes. In this chapter, you will learn about three kinds of communities. They are called **urban**, **rural**, and **suburban**.

2.1 Cities Are Urban Communities

Cities have lots of buildings and people. People often walk from place to place in a city. Sometimes they take a bus or a taxi. Many people ride trains from one part of a city to another. Some people drive cars.

Many people live in apartments in cities. One apartment building might have 50 or more homes. Have you ever been to a city?

2.2 Living in Urban Communities

Cities are exciting. There are many stores and restaurants in a city. There are parks, playgrounds, and museums.

Sometimes, cities are noisy. Cars honk their horns. People sing. Babies cry. Dogs bark.

There are crowds in a city. There are lots of people on the sidewalks. Stores and restaurants are busy places, too. What do you like about cities?

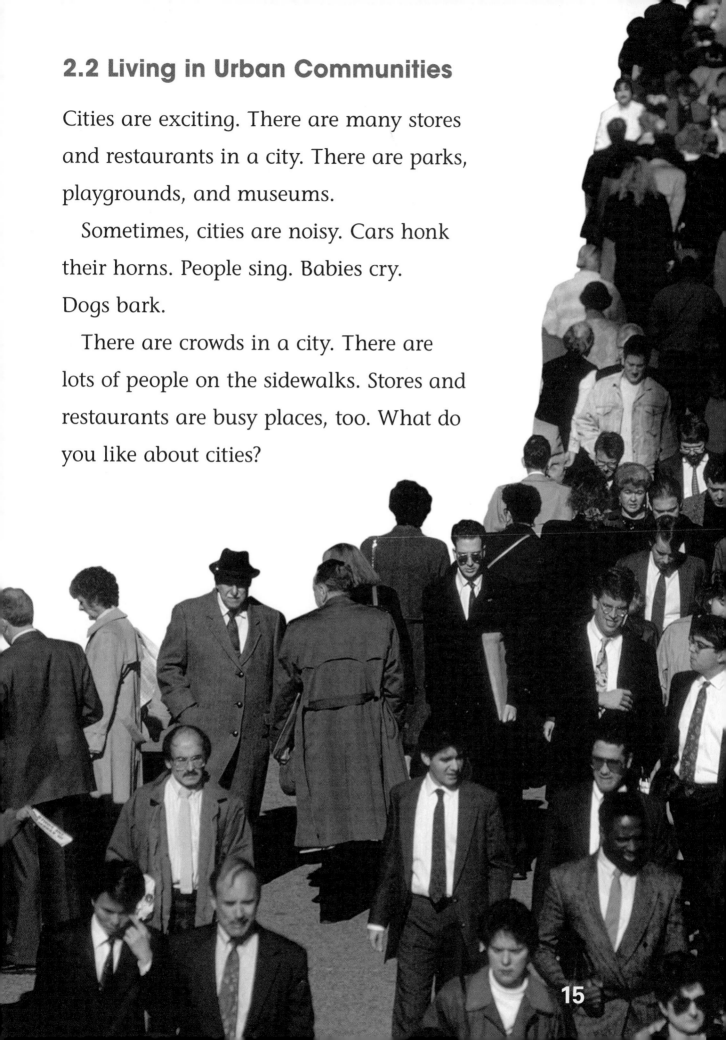

2.3 Small Towns Are Rural Communities

Small towns are in the countryside. They are far from cities.

Small towns have fewer people than cities. Many people know their neighbors well in a small town.

Small towns might have just one store. There may be a post office, a bank, and a school. Do you live in a small town?

2.4 Living in Rural Communities

Many people live and work on farms in rural communities. They drive to the store and the post office. Students ride a bus to school.

There are different ways to have fun in a small town. In a city, you might visit a big aquarium. In a small town, you might go fishing. What things would you like to do in a small town?

2.5 Communities Outside Cities Are Suburbs

Suburbs are smaller communities just outside of cities. Many people live in suburbs. Suburbs have many kinds of homes. They have schools, fire stations, police stations, and hospitals.

Suburbs have stores and gas stations. They have parks and other places to play. Do you live in a suburb?

18

2.6 Living in Suburban Communities

Many families live in suburbs. Some people live in houses. Some people live in apartments. Lots of homes have yards.

Most people drive cars in a suburb. People drive to work. They drive to shopping malls. There are lots of parking lots in suburbs. What else might you see in a suburb?

Summary

Urban communities are cities with many people. Rural communities are small towns far from cities. Suburban communities lie just outside of cities.

Instant Suburbs

About 60 years ago, Bill Levitt had an idea. He wanted to build homes for young families. Thousands of homes! How did his new idea help form suburbs around the country?

Up and down the street, workers were building new houses. They worked very quickly. They could finish about thirty houses in a day. All the houses looked almost the same.

The town was called Levittown, Pennsylvania. Hal and Sylvia Lefcourt bought one of the new houses. Sylvia was so happy she cried. Hal said he always dreamed of owning a house.

This suburb used to be farmland.

Families moved to the new suburbs.

What was so special about Levittown?

During the 1940s, there was a world war. When it ended, millions of U.S. soldiers came home. They had young families. They needed houses to live in.

Bill Levitt and his family had farmland near New York City. They planned a suburb there. They built new houses faster than anyone had before. Then they sold the houses at a low price. They called the community Levittown.

The new suburb was very popular. The Levitts built two more Levittowns. One suburb was in Pennsylvania. The other suburb was in New Jersey.

Levittowns were built near highways. People could drive easily to work in nearby cities.

The houses were small and modern. Everything was new. Some homes came with a recent invention—a TV!

The houses had huge windows in the living room. These big windows were called "picture windows." Parents could watch their children playing outside.

There were lots of children, too. They played in the backyards. Because no fences were allowed in Levittowns, children ran from yard to yard.

Levittown houses looked almost alike.

Levittown houses look very different today.

The Levitts also built playgrounds, stores, and community centers. They built whole towns from start to finish.

Some people did not like the Levittowns. They said everything looked the same. They did not like the rules the Levitts made. Some rules said what you could do and not do to the houses. Other rules said who could buy houses and who could not.

Still, the "instant suburbs" were popular. Other builders copied the Levitts' ideas in new suburbs across the country. Later, people made changes to the Levitt houses, but the suburbs still exist today.

JOE'S DELI

CITY PARK

KEY

Merry-go-round	
Picnic area	
Play-ground	
Rest rooms	
Sand area	
Swan boats	

NORTH

YOU ARE HERE

ICE CREAM

How Do We Use Maps?

Maps come in all shapes and sizes. A map is a drawing of a place or a community. It can show any area of Earth.

A map shows what a place looks like from above. Maps have different tools that people can use to find their way. You will learn to use these tools to read a map.

Washington, D.C.

Washington, D.C. Map

3.1 A Map Shows a Place

A map is a drawing of a place from above. The map is smaller than the place. A map shows important things in the place. It does not show everything in that place.

Look at the picture of the city above. Now look at the map of that city.

Which things from the picture does the map show?

3.2 A Map Has a Key

Some keys open doors. Other keys are clues about new things. A **map key** explains pictures and colors on a map. A map key is also called a legend.

The pictures and colors on a map are called **symbols**. The map key tells us what these symbols mean.

How many kinds of symbols do you see on this map?

Farm

Farm Map

MAP KEY
☐ Farm Building
▲ Barn
🌳 Tree
━ Road
☐ Field

27

3.3 A Map Has a Grid

A **map grid** is a set of lines that cross each other. The lines make squares all over the map. Each row has a letter. Each column has a number.

The grid helps us find places on the map. We can follow a letter and a number to find squares on the grid.

Look at the grid on this map. What is in Square A2?

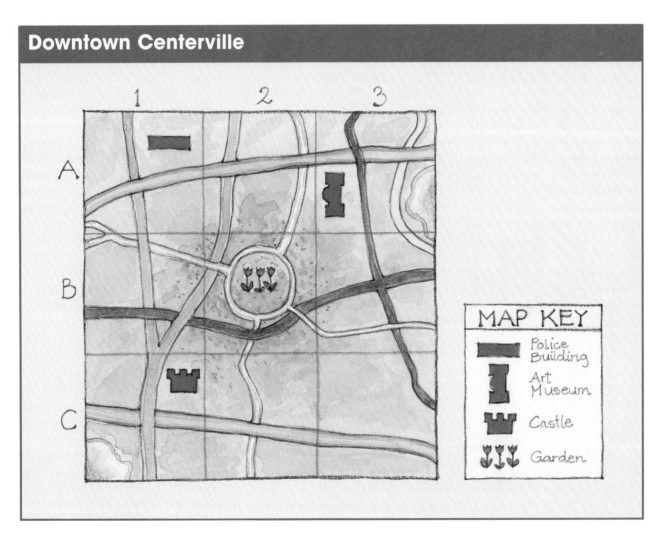

Downtown Centerville

MAP KEY

Police Building

Art Museum

Castle

Garden

3.4 A Map Has a Compass Rose

A **compass** points to the directions north, south, east, and west. A **compass rose** is a drawing of a compass on a map. It shows the directions on a map.

Look at this map. Which building is north of the hospital?

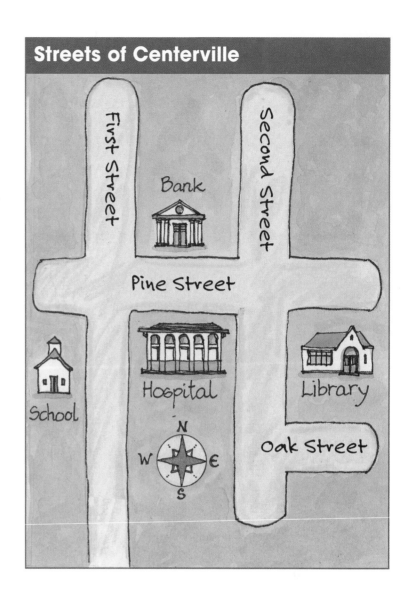

Streets of Centerville

Summary

A map shows what places look like from above. A map has a key to explain symbols. A map can have a grid. A map can have a compass rose. People use maps to help them find their way.

Mapping a Trip

When you want to get from here to there, a map is the tool for you. When you want to find a special place, a map helps then, too. How did one family figure out what maps show and how to use them?

Rosie and Chris Carto were very excited. The Carto family was taking a trip to Washington, D.C.

"Where is Washington, D.C.?" Rosie asked.

"It's somewhere on Earth. I know that!" Chris answered.

Can Chris and Rosie see Washington, D.C.?

"Hmmm," Rosie said. "So, let's look at Earth to find it."

"Don't be silly," Chris laughed. "How can we look at the whole Earth?"

"I'm not silly. We can use a globe. A globe is a model of the Earth. Look at this!" Rosie said.

Rosie and Chris spun the globe. "Here is the United States," Rosie pointed. "Let's find Washington, D.C."

Cities looked very small on the globe. Rosie found Washington, D.C. A star symbol showed that it was our nation's capital city.

Rosie and Chris live in Sacramento. It is a city in California. "Wow," Chris said. "We live in the western United States. Washington, D.C. is in the eastern part of the country."

"I want to see the Capitol more than anything," Rosie said. "The Capitol is the building where people make laws for our country. Can you find it on this globe?"

"You can't find a building on a globe!" Chris laughed. "We need a map."

Rosie said, "Here is a map of the United States. I see Sacramento and Washington, D.C. But I can't find the Capitol building."

Why can't Rosie find the Capitol on this map?

Map Scale

INCHES

MILES

Chris looked at the **map scale**. A map scale shows distance on the map. One inch on the map equaled 300 miles. He used it to find the real distance on Earth. Chris said, "Washington, D.C. is about 2,400 miles away. It will take us many days to drive there."

Just then, Mr. and Mrs. Carto came in. "Don't worry, we are taking a plane," Mrs. Carto said.

This scale tells how much space the map shows.

A week later, the Carto family was in Washington, D.C. Mr. Carto bought a map of the city. He pointed to a symbol on the map. "Here is the Capitol building," he said. "Let's take the subway to get there."

The Cartos used another map to find their way on the subway. Then they walked to the National Mall. The National Mall is a long park. Many important buildings are on the National Mall.

The Cartos used a city map to find the Capitol.

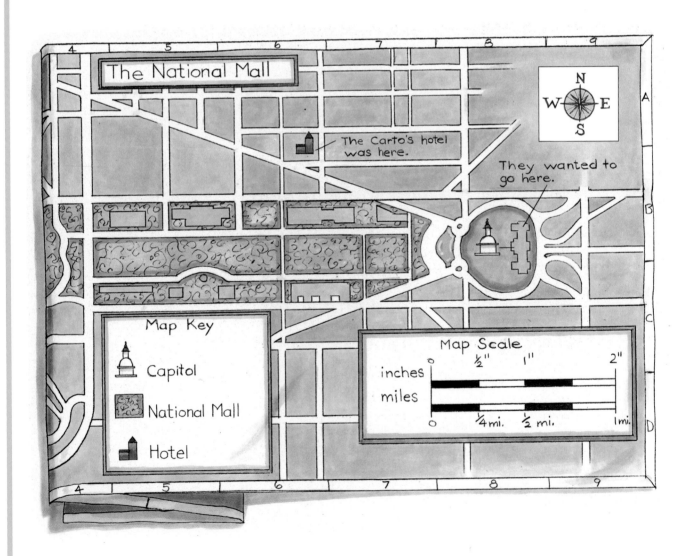

Everyone studied the map of Washington, D.C. Chris found the National Mall on the map. "We are here," he said. "Let's find the Capitol."

"Is it near or far from where we are?" Rosie asked. She was very excited.

Rosie looked at the map, too. "Here is the Capitol," she said, "It is east of where we are. Let's go!"

At last, Rosie stood in front of the Capitol. "We used a lot of maps to get here," she said, "but it was worth it!"

Rosie shows the globe and maps her family used.

35

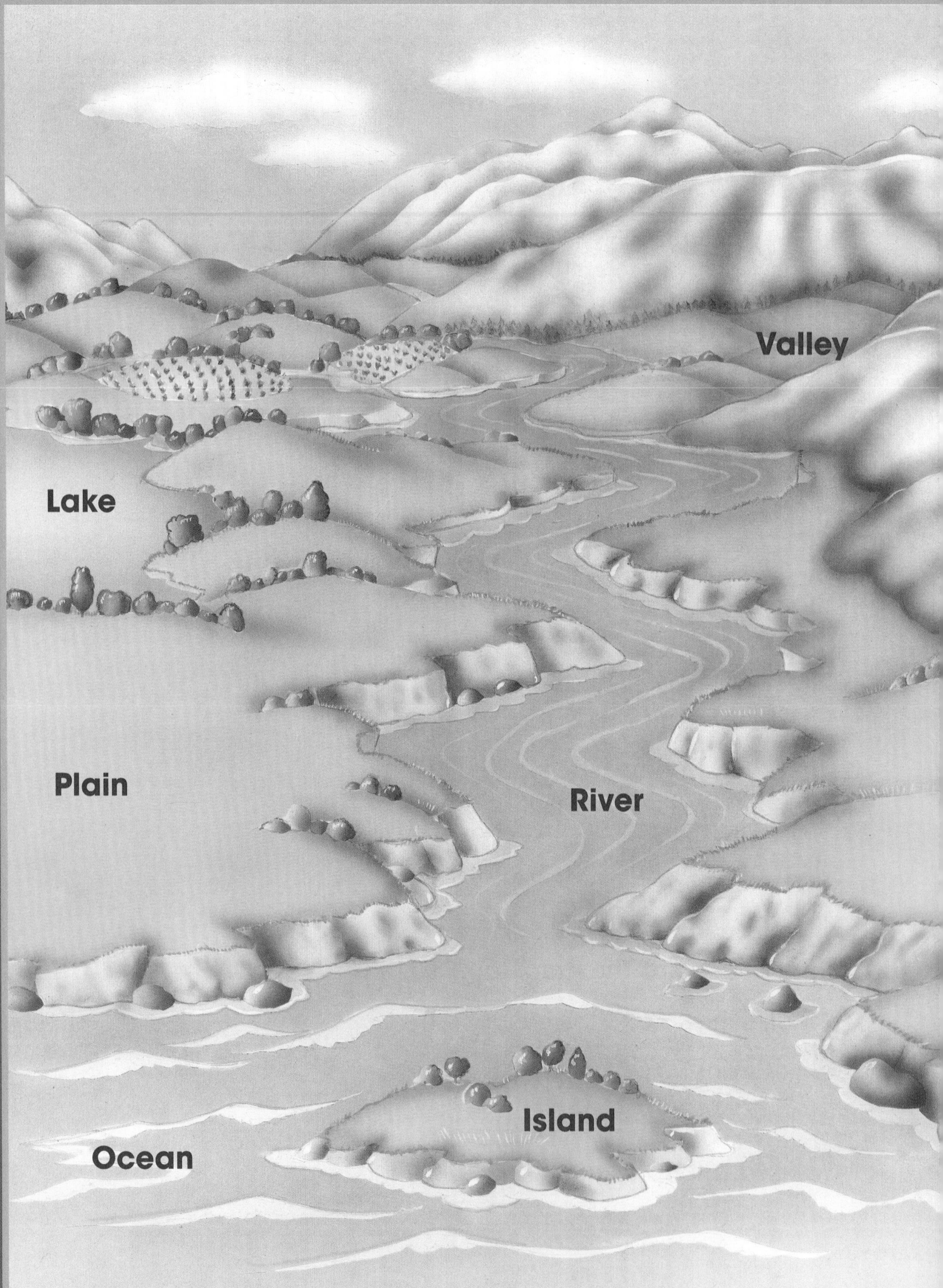

Valley

Lake

Plain

River

Ocean

Island

Mountains

Desert

What Is Geography?

Earth has many places and people. **Geography** is the study of our planet—its land, water, and people.

The geography of a community is important to the people who live there. Geography affects how the people live, work, and play.

In this chapter, you will study the geography of different places. You will also learn how people use maps to study geography.

Mountains

4.1 Mountains and Valleys

Mountains are the tallest kind of land on Earth. Mountains have many trees. It snows on mountains in the winter.

Valleys are low places that lie between mountains. Most valleys have **rivers**. A river is a body of fresh water that moves through land. Snow melts off the mountains and fills the rivers.

There are communities on mountains. There are communities in valleys. Do you live near mountains and valleys?

Valley

4.2 Deserts and Plains

Deserts are dry places that get very little rain. Deserts get very hot during the day. Deserts are not good places to grow crops. People in desert communities learn not to waste water.

Desert

Plains are large areas of flat land. Plains get more rain than deserts. Plains are good places for farms that grow crops and raise animals. Are there farms and plains where you live?

Plain

4.3 Rivers and Lakes

Rivers bring water to farms, towns, and cities. Some rivers flow right through communities. Rivers can also connect communities. People and goods can travel on rivers.

River

Lakes are bodies of water with land all around them. Rain, rivers, and melting snow bring water to lakes. Lakes can be big or small.

Lots of people like living near lakes and rivers. They can go fishing, swimming, and boating. Do you live near a river or lake?

Lake

Ocean

4.4 Oceans and Islands

An **island** is land with water all around it. There are islands in lakes and in **oceans**. Oceans have salty water. They are the largest bodies of water on Earth.

Island

Some islands are small places. They don't have everything that people need. Ships and airplanes bring goods to islands. Have you ever been to an island?

4.5 Physical Maps

Geographers use many kinds of maps to study Earth and its people. One kind is a physical map.

Physical maps show land and bodies of water. They use colors and symbols to show mountains, plains, and deserts. You can also find rivers, lakes, and oceans on this kind of map.

What kinds of land and water do you see on the map below?

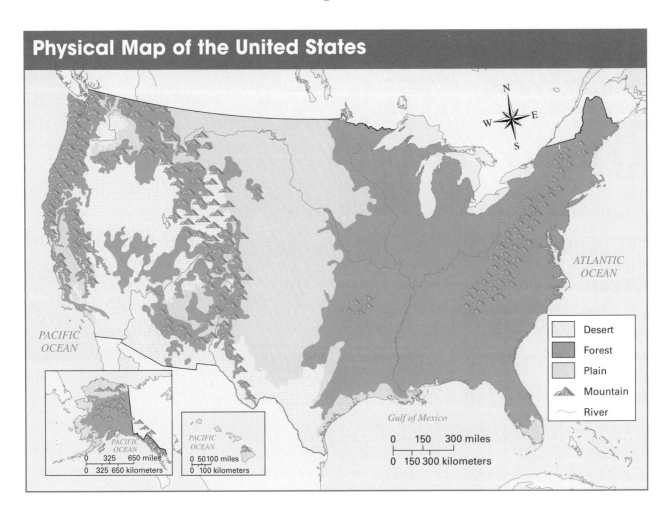

Physical Map of the United States

ATLANTIC OCEAN

PACIFIC OCEAN

Gulf of Mexico

PACIFIC OCEAN

PACIFIC OCEAN

0   325   650 miles
0   325 650 kilometers

0 50100 miles
0   100 kilometers

0   150   300 miles
0   150 300 kilometers

Desert
Forest
Plain
Mountain
River

4.6 Other Kinds of Maps

People use maps to find places and things. Some maps show streets. Some maps show states and countries. Others show crops or numbers of people in different areas. There are even maps that show the weather. How are the people in the picture above using their map?

Summary

Geography is the study of Earth's land, water, and people. Communities have different geography. Geography affects how people live, work, and play. Physical maps can show features of geography.

Riding for Climate

Is the geography of Earth changing? Many people say *yes* because the climate is changing. Climate is the weather in a place over time. How are two men showing why climate matters?

David Kroodsma and Bill Bradlee were worried. Earth is getting warmer. This could cause big problems, they said. Deserts could grow. There could be more floods or droughts. A drought is a long time without rain. Some plants and animals might die out. Oceans could rise. Some islands and cities might be under water.

What could people do to keep Earth from getting too warm? David and Bill had some ideas. To share them, they biked across the country. They called their trip "Ride for Climate USA."

David and Bill started in Massachusetts.

44

David and Bill like to ride across plains.

Climate Change

David and Bill wanted to tell people how a warmer planet makes climates change. These changes can hurt people, animals, and plants.

Why did they ride bikes? Bikes don't use gasoline. Cars burn a lot of gasoline. That makes Earth warmer. So using less gasoline will help Earth. David and Bill told people to help by biking more and driving less. They told people biking is good for you, too.

David and Bill also told people about cars that use less gasoline. They talked about light bulbs that use less energy. They explained how to make power from the wind and sun. All these ideas could stop Earth from getting too much warmer.

Some children help "ride for climate."

Crossing the Continent

This map shows the trip David and Bill took in 2007. Put your finger on X. This is Boston, where they began their route. Follow the red line to trace the trip. Find the Y. This is San Francisco. David and Bill ended their trip there. They rode across North America.

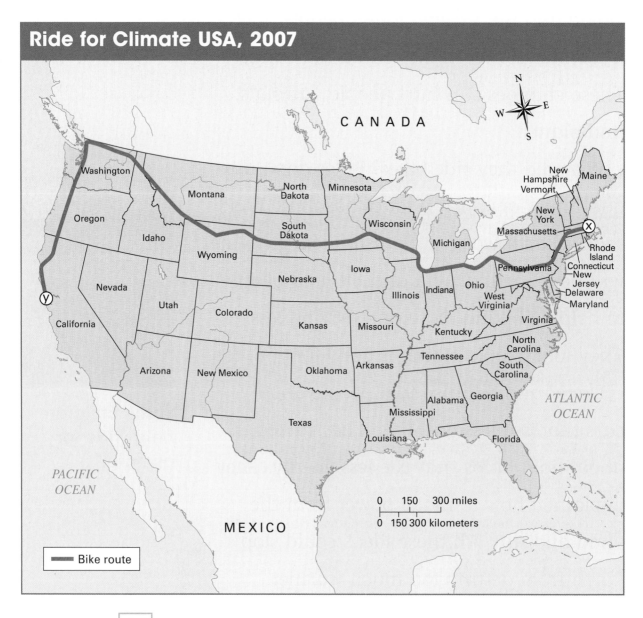

Ride for Climate USA, 2007

Bike route

The United States is our country. Canada is the country north of us. Mexico is the country south of us.

These three countries make up North America. North America is a **continent**. Continents are the seven largest land areas on Earth.

David and Bill rode on flat plains and high mountain roads. Some days they rode in forests. Other days they rode through desert. They rode in sun, rain, and even snowstorms. They saw how geography and climate change from place to place.

Riding on hot days was tough!

In each place, David and Bill knew climate change could happen. They told their ideas about stopping Earth from getting warmer to many people. Together we can protect our planet, they said.

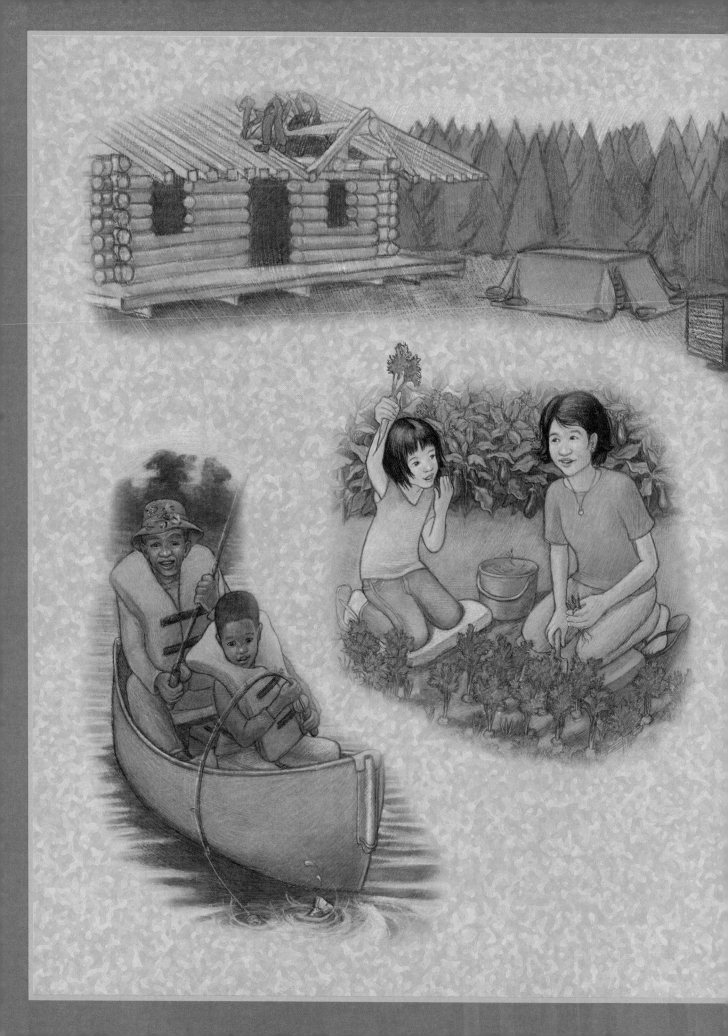

How Do People Use Our Environment?

We call everything around us our **environment**. Land is part of our environment. So are plants and animals. They are all part of nature too.

In this chapter, you will learn about some environments. You will see how people use things from nature. You will learn that people can hurt their environment, too.

5.1 Nature Is Important to Us

Plants and animals are part of nature. So are trees and stones. So are water and air.

People use nature for things they need and want. They use plants and animals for food and clothing. They use trees and stones for houses. People breathe air and drink water. Things in nature that people use are called **natural resources**.

Look all around you. What things are part of nature? What things are made by people?

5.2 We Live in Many Different Environments

Different environments have different land and weather. They have different plants and animals.

Some places have mountains. Some have deserts. Some have rivers or oceans.

Some places have hot weather. Some are cold. Some are wet. Some are dry.

People live in different ways in different places. They work and play in different ways.

Look all around you. What is your environment like?

5.3 Using Nature for Food

We use plants and animals for food. Different foods come from different environments.

Fish live in oceans, lakes, and rivers. Cows live in grassy places. We raise pigs, sheep, and chickens for food.

Farmers grow crops for food. Some crops, like wheat, grow well on the plains. There the weather is hot and dry. Other plants need rainy environments.

Look around you. What kind of food could you catch, gather, or grow in your environment?

5.4 Using Nature for Clothing

We use plants and animals to make clothing. Cotton comes from a plant. It grows only where the climate is warm. People weave cotton threads into cloth.

Woolen cloth comes from the hair of sheep and other animals. People spin the hairs into yarn. The yarn is used to make warm clothes.

Look around you. What clothing comes from the plants and animals in your environment?

5.5 Using Nature to Make Shelter

We use nature to make shelter.

People use wood to make homes. Wood comes from trees in the forest.

People use stones to build homes. Stones come from many different places.

People also use the soil to make homes. In the desert, they mix mud with straw to make bricks.

Look around you. What could you use to make shelter in your environment?

5.6 Polluting Our Water

Sometimes people don't take good care of Earth's water.

They throw trash in rivers, lakes, and streams. They let poisons spill in the ocean. When they do this, they are polluting the water. To **pollute** means to hurt the environment.

Water pollution is very harmful. People can't drink the water. They can't swim in it. Fish and other animals may die.

What can you do to help keep our water clean and safe?

5.7 Spoiling Our Land

Sometimes people don't take good care of Earth's land.

They cut down too many trees. They dump trash on the land. They bury poisons in the soil. This is called land pollution.

We share the land with plants and animals. When we spoil the land, plants cannot grow. Animals may die because they have no food or home.

What can you do to help keep the land clean and beautiful?

5.8 Polluting Our Air

Sometimes people don't take good care of
the air.

Factories and cars fill the air with smoke.
This is called air pollution.

Dirty air is hard for people to breathe.
Animals can get sick, too.

What things can you do to help keep the
air clean?

Summary

Our environment is all around us. We get food
from it. We also get clothing and shelter. When we
pollute, it hurts people, plants, and animals. We all
need clean water, land, and air.

Using Plants in New Ways

What can you get from peanuts beside peanut butter? Sometimes people come up with new ways to use plants. George Washington Carver did. How did he use plants to change people's lives?

George Washington Carver loved plants. When he was a little boy, about 150 years ago, he lived on a farm.

There were plants in the fields. There were plants in the woods nearby. Little George loved to study them. He loved to draw them too.

George left home before he was a teenager. He wanted to go to a better school. Everywhere, he tried to learn more about plants.

This statue shows Carver as a boy.

58

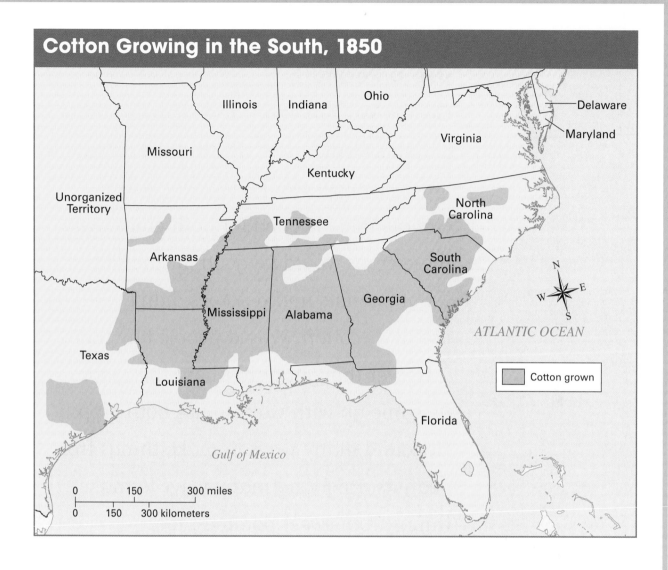

Cotton Growing in the South, 1850

Illinois
Indiana
Ohio
Delaware
Maryland
Missouri
Virginia
Kentucky
Unorganized Territory
North Carolina
Tennessee
Arkansas
South Carolina
Mississippi
Alabama
Georgia
ATLANTIC OCEAN
Texas
Louisiana
Cotton grown
Florida
Gulf of Mexico

0   150   300 miles
0   150   300 kilometers

When George grew up, he taught at a college. It was in Alabama. Its name was Tuskegee Institute. There, George kept studying plants.

At that time, farmers in the South grew cotton. Loads of cotton! But growing only one kind of plant was bad for the soil.

Carver wanted to help the farmers. He wanted to help the environment. So that's what he did.

59

How Many Ways Can We Use a Peanut?

George Washington Carver learned that peanuts would grow well in the South. Sweet potatoes would, too. The warm climate there is good for both crops. And these crops would be good for the soil.

But peanuts and potatoes didn't seem as useful as cotton. Would people buy them?

Carver thought hard about this. Soon, he came up with ways to use both crops. He found many ways to make things from peanuts. He found many ways to make things from sweet potatoes, too.

Find some of those things on this chart.

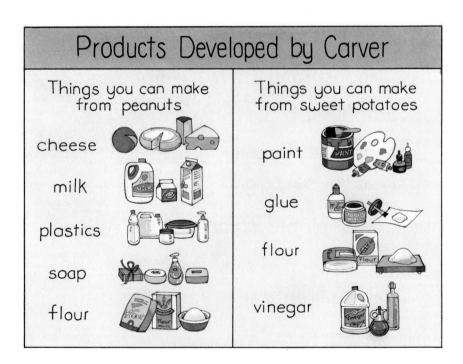

Products Developed by Carver

Things you can make from peanuts	Things you can make from sweet potatoes
cheese	paint
milk	glue
plastics	flour
soap	vinegar
flour	

George Washington Carver changed how people farmed. Farmers grew new crops. They sold crops for more money. They used the money to buy new things.

Carver never stopped teaching. He wrote letters on ways to use plants. He visited farms and schools.

Later, he gave all his money to Tuskegee. He wanted students to find more uses for plants. Students still study plants at Tuskegee today.

Carver teaches his students.

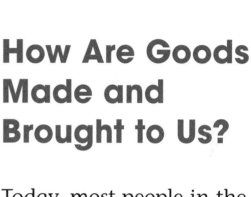

How Are Goods Made and Brought to Us?

Today, most people in the United States do not grow their own food. They do not make their own clothes. Instead, they buy them.

In this chapter, you will learn how **goods** are grown on farms and made in factories. Goods are things that can be bought, sold, and traded. Then, you will read about the different ways that goods travel to stores.

6.1 Farmers Grow Our Food

Farmers grow most of our food for us. Some farmers grow wheat. Some farmers grow corn. Some farmers grow tomatoes.

Some farms are small. Other farms are large, with lots of land for growing crops.

Some farms are near the ocean. Other farms are in the middle of the country.

What different foods can you name that grow on farms?

6.2 People Make Many Goods in Factories

Most of our other goods, like toys and clothing, are made in factories.

Factories often have large machines. They use many workers. Each worker does one small part of the whole job. Together, they make lots of goods.

What things can you name that come from factories?

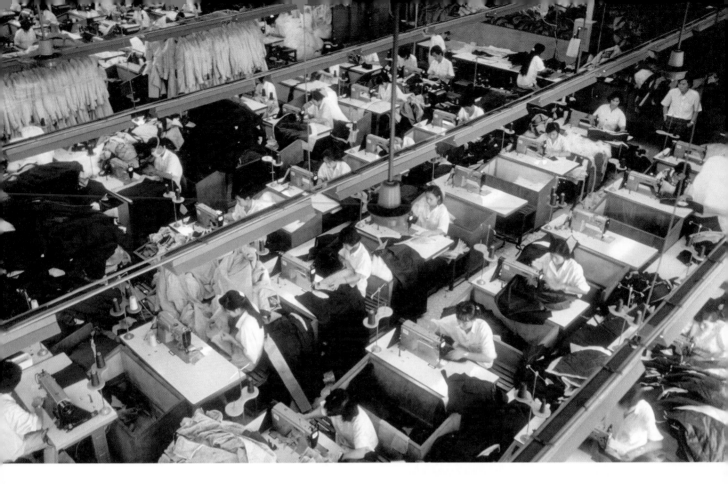

6.3 A Busy Shirt Factory

It takes many workers to make one shirt.

One worker cuts shirt pieces from cloth. Another sews the pieces together. A third worker sews on buttons. Another makes buttonholes. Other workers add pockets and labels.

At the end, one person makes sure that the shirt is perfect. Then, it is ready to be ironed and wrapped.

How many workers do you think made the clothes you are wearing?

6.4 How Goods Are Brought to Stores

Goods are loaded onto trucks at farms and at factories. The trucks take the goods to warehouses. The goods stay there until it is time for them to be brought to stores.

To bring goods to stores, people use many different kinds of **transportation**. For example, some goods travel in planes. Some goods cross oceans in ships. Some goods travel by train. Some goods are driven in trucks.

How do you think the goods in your home were brought to stores?

6.5 From Around the World to Our Community

All over the world, people grow and make the goods we need and want.

Some goods come from India. Some goods come from Japan. Goods come from many countries. We use transportation to move goods from one place to another.

Can you name any goods that are made in other countries?

6.6 From the Store to You

We buy some goods we need and want in stores.

There are many kinds of stores. Some stores sell food. Some stores sell clothes. Some stores sell toys. Many stores sell lots of different things.

Can you name different kinds of stores in your community?

Summary

We buy most of the goods we need and want. Farmers grow food for us. Factory workers make goods for us. Goods travel to stores by planes, ships, trains, and trucks. We buy food, clothes, toys, and other goods at stores in our community.

Food from the Desert

Southeast California is mostly desert. But it has many farms. How do people raise crops in such a dry place?

The Colorado River begins high in the Rocky Mountains. It flows south and west through many states. It ends in the Gulf of California.

Near its end, the river flows through a valley. For thousands of years, the river often flooded. The floods left a layer of rich dirt on the land.

The Colorado River flows through a valley.

Parts of the valley are still very dry. It rains only about 3 inches in a whole year.

People Come to the Valley

Hundreds of years ago, American Indians passed through the valley. They planted seeds in the rich dirt. Later, they came back to gather their crops. They grew vegetables such as beans and corn.

Later, people from Spain and Mexico came to the valley. They thought the valley was too hot and dry to farm. So they moved on.

Bringing Water to the Valley

Things began to change in the early 1900s.

More and more people moved to California. They thought the valley would be a good place to grow crops. But the crops needed more water.

People thought the Colorado River could help their crops. Workers built canals to carry water from the river into the valley. A **canal** is a waterway made by people. Canals can bring water to places that need it.

Can you find the canal that brings water to the Imperial Valley?

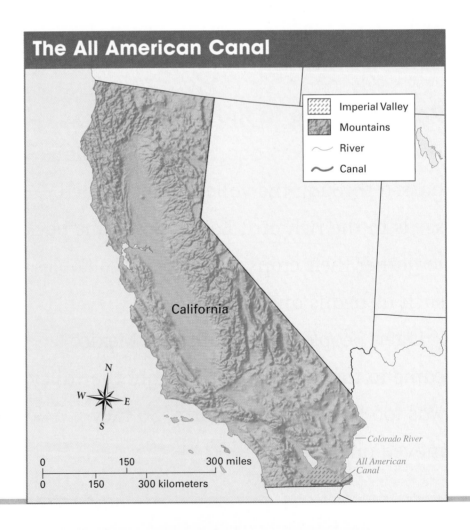

The All American Canal

Imperial Valley
Mountains
River
Canal

California

N
W   E
S

Colorado River

All American Canal

0   150   300 miles
0   150   300 kilometers

Crops are picked, transported, and sold in stores.

After the canals were built, people started large farms. They also gave the valley a new name—the Imperial Valley.

Today, the Imperial Valley has some of the best farmland in the United States. Farmers grow many kinds of vegetables and fruits. They sell them to stores and factories.

Farmers ship food out of the valley on trucks. They ship it on trains. They ship it on airplanes, too. People all over the country eat these farm goods.

Each year, farmers from the Imperial Valley grow about one billion dollars worth of crops. What a lot of food!

The Imperial Valley and Yogurt

Do you like yogurt? Do you know where it comes from?

We use cow's milk to make yogurt. Eating a plant called alfalfa helps the cows make that milk. And guess what? The Imperial Valley is the largest region that grows alfalfa in the world.

Farmers in the valley transport the alfalfa hay to dairy farms. California cows eat most of it.

Most dairy farmers milk their cows every day. They put much of the milk in big tanks on milk trucks. The trucks bring the milk to dairy factories. Some of the milk goes to yogurt factories.

These cows live on a farm in the Imperial Valley.

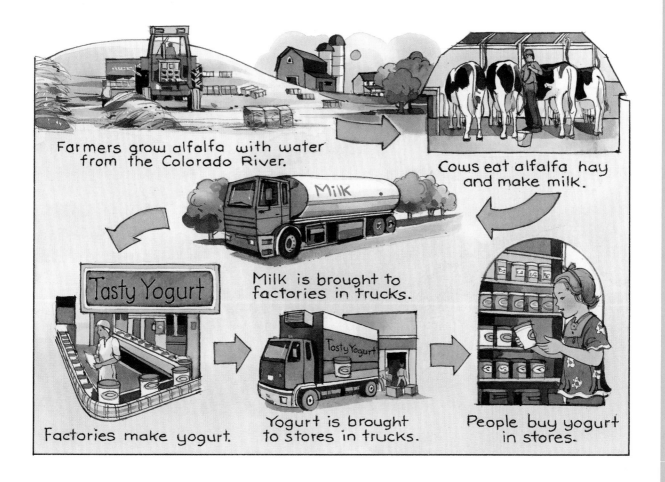

Farmers grow alfalfa with water from the Colorado River.

Cows eat alfalfa hay and make milk.

Milk is brought to factories in trucks.

Tasty Yogurt

Factories make yogurt.

Yogurt is brought to stores in trucks.

People buy yogurt in stores.

There, workers warm the milk. They add a special ingredient to help the milk form curds. Curds are lumps. The workers also add bacteria to make the yogurt. Sometimes they put in fruit and nuts.

The yogurt is shipped to grocery stores on refrigerated trucks. People all over the country eat yogurt made from milk that came from the Imperial Valley!

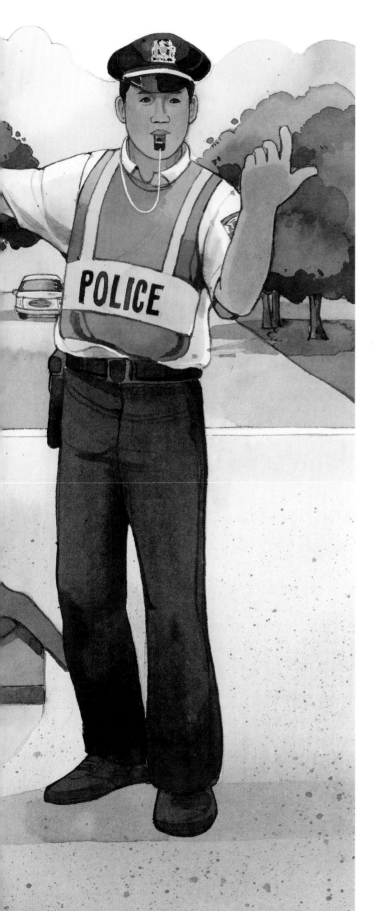

Who Provides Services in a Community?

You have learned about jobs where people make goods. There are other kinds of jobs too. In these jobs, people help other people. Different ways of helping are called **services**.

In this chapter, you will learn about the people who provide services in the community.

7.1 People Who Give Us Ideas

Some people give us ideas.

Authors share ideas by writing. They might write books, plays, or poems.

TV reporters bring us news and ideas. They go to places where the news is happening. Then they talk about it on TV.

Architects have ideas about what a building will look like. They draw their ideas on a piece of paper. They call their drawing a blueprint.

Can you think of other jobs like these?

7.2 People Who Fix Things

Some people fix things.

Plumbers put water pipes into buildings. They also fix pipes when they break.

Electricians work with electricity. They put electric wires in buildings. They also repair things that use electricity.

Mechanics fix cars when they break down. They change tires that are flat or worn out. They put new parts in our cars.

Can you think of other jobs like these?

7.3 People Who Take Care of Us and Our Pets

Some people take care of people or pets.

Childcare workers take care of children when their parents are working.

Doctors help people stay healthy. If we are sick, a doctor tells us ways to get better.

Our pets have their own doctors. They are called veterinarians. They take care of sick or hurt animals.

Can you think of other jobs like these?

7.4 People Who Take Care of Our Community

Many people work hard to care for our community.

Police officers keep our community safe. They help people obey the community's laws. A **law** is a rule. Police officers stop people who do not obey laws.

Firefighters put out fires. They rescue people from danger. Some firefighters have extra training. They help people who are hurt or sick.

Mail carriers deliver letters and packages. They bring mail to homes and businesses.

Rangers keep parks and forests safe and clean. They also teach people about the plants and animals that live there.

Summary

Some people provide services. They give us ideas. They fix things. They care for people and animals. They keep us safe. They care for our parks and forests.

Caring for Central Park

People work together to provide services in a community. It takes many workers to care for a large city park. Who takes care of New York City's Central Park?

"Working in Central Park is like coming home," Maria Hernandez says. "I grew up in this park. It has been my playground since I was a child."

Maria takes care of everything that grows in the park. That's a big job. Thousands of trees grow in the park. There are many kinds of flowers. Lots of grass grows in the park, too.

Central Park gives people in the city a lot of room to have fun.

Luckily for Maria, lots of workers help care for the park. They all have the same goal. They want the park to be a safe and happy place. They want everyone to enjoy its beauty.

Many workers care for Central Park's flowers and trees.

Maria helps the gardeners plant flowers and water the plants.

She talks with planners. They share ideas about things to change in the park.

Maria works with volunteers. Together they fix things in the park.

Sometimes there are concerts in the park. Thousands of people sit on the grass. Maria tells the workers how to protect the lawns.

Maria helps care for the birds that live in Central Park. One day, a baby bird could not fly from its nest. Its leg was caught in a piece of string. An Urban Park Ranger called Maria. Together, they freed the bird and took it to an animal hospital.

Birds are not the only animals in the park. Thousands of dogs love to play in Central Park. Maria works with the dog owners. She helps them follow the rules.

Everyone can enjoy the park.

Dog owners help keep the park safe, clean, and fun!

Children do community service projects in the park. Maria wants children to learn about the park. "I want kids to know that the park is more than a playground," she said. "I want them to learn how to take care of this special place."

Maria loves her job in Central Park. "It makes me feel good to know that people have confidence in me," she said. "I love working with people. And I love working with living things. At the end of the day, I can see that I have made something better."

How Can I Be a Good Shopper?

People use money to buy the things they **need** and **want**. Needs are things people must have to live. Wants are things people would like to have but don't need to live. People make choices about what to buy when they shop.

In this chapter, you will learn how to make good decisions when you go shopping.

8.1 We Need Money to Buy Things

We all need money to buy goods and services. Most people earn money by making goods or doing a service. People decide how they spend their own money.

People spend money to buy things they need. Sometimes they spend money to buy things they want. People also **save** money to use in the future. That means people put away some of their money and do not spend it right away.

How do you spend and save your money?

8.2 We Make Choices When We Shop

We go shopping to buy the things we need and want. Shopping can be fun.

However, shopping is not always easy. We cannot buy everything we see. We must make choices.

Some choices are about money. Should you buy a drink or a toy? Some choices are about time. Is there enough time to get a haircut?

How do you make choices?

8.3 We Buy What We Need

There is a difference between what we need and what we want.

People need food. People need clothing. People need shelter. People sometimes want things they don't need. You may want lots of toys. You may need a new pair of shoes.

We make a good choice when we buy the things we need first.

What things do you need? What things do you want?

8.4 We Are Good Shoppers

How can you be a good shopper? Here are some hints.

Shop for needs before wants.

Look for goods that are made well.

Look in a few stores for the best price.

Keep your sales receipt. If something is wrong with what you buy, you may be able to return it to the store.

How are you a good shopper?

Summary

People use money to buy things. They also save money for later. People shop for goods and services. Good shoppers buy what they need first. Then they buy the things they want.

Shopping for School

School celebrations are a lot of fun, and a lot of work. They also can cost money. What does it take to be a good shopper for your school?

Every year Jackie Robinson Elementary School had a school fair. This year it was called Celebrate Our World! Students wanted to share how people around the world are alike and different.

Count the faces in the graph to see how the class voted.

The second grade class was asked to make some food for the fair. Students had different ideas about what to make. How could they decide? The class talked about how each plan could work. Then they voted.

	Bake pies	Cook rice	Bake bread
1	☺	☺	☺
2	☺	☺	☺
3	☺	☺	☺
4	☺	☺	☺
5	☺	☺	
6	☺	☺	
7		☺	
8		☺	
9		☺	
10		☺	

The students needed money to pay for the food. They earned $45 by washing cars. Their teacher, Mrs. Marino, put the money in the bank.

Next, the students planned their dishes. One team would make rice and beans from Mexico. One team would make fried rice from China. One team would make rice pilaf from Pakistan.

The teams listed what they needed to make each dish. Mrs. Marino helped them make a **budget**. A budget is a plan for how to spend and save money. Each team had $15 to buy the ingredients for its dish.

Now the class was ready to shop.

"Let's go to the grocery store," Mrs. Marino said.

Darrell's team shopped for the fried rice. They had a problem. Snow peas were too expensive for their budget. If they bought snow peas, they could not buy other items. They decided to buy regular peas instead.

Latisha's team shopped for the rice and beans. They found a can of beans from Mexico on sale.

The students took their lists to the store.

"These are special," Latisha said. "They are on sale, so we can afford to buy other things we need."

Rice and Beans
Rice
Refried Beans
Salsa
Oil

Fried Rice
Rice
Green Onions
Celery
Carrots
Snow Peas
Oil

Rice Pilaf
Rice
Dried apricots
Sliced almonds
Onions
Oil

The students were good shoppers.

At the checkout counter, each team paid for what it bought. The students counted out their money carefully. They counted their change. They asked for receipts.

The second graders spent $38.50 on their groceries. They had $6.50 left over. Mrs. Marino put their change in the bank. They could use that money for other projects.

The class felt good about their shopping. They had made good choices. They were careful with their money.

"Now it's time to cook," Mrs. Marino said. And that is just what they did!

How Do Communities Change?

Sometimes communities grow bigger. Sometimes communities get smaller.

In this chapter, you will look at how two cities changed over time. You will see how people made their cities better places to live.

9.1 Communities Change over Time

Communities grow bigger when people move to them. Communities get smaller when people move away from them.

People move to a community for many reasons. Some people come for a new job. Some people want to live in a different home.

People move away from communities for many reasons, too. Some people change jobs. Some people want to live in a different town.

9.2 People Move to a Community

Look at this picture of a steel mill in Pittsburgh, Pennsylvania. Many people moved to Pittsburgh to work in this mill.

The new people needed many things. They needed homes. They needed stores. They needed schools for their children.

People built new buildings and other places. The community grew bigger.

9.3 People Move Away from a Community

One day, the steel mill closed. Many people moved away from Pittsburgh.

Some of the stores closed. Some of the buildings were left empty.

No one took care of the empty buildings. They started to fall apart. The photograph below shows how one neighborhood looked.

9.4 People Work to Make Their Communities Better

Some people wanted to make Pittsburgh beautiful again. They fixed old buildings. They built new places. They wanted people to move back to their city.

The photograph shows Pittsburgh today. What changes do you see?

Summary

Communities grow bigger as people move to them. Communities get smaller as people move away. Some people make their communities better. They fix old buildings. They build new places. They care about their communities.

Los Angeles Grows

Los Angeles is a huge, busy city. But long ago it was mostly farmland. Cows grazed where buildings now sit. How did this community grow and change?

At first, most people in the town farmed.

In 1781, people from Mexico built a farming town where Los Angeles stands now. They named the new community "El Pueblo de la Reyna de los Ángeles." This means "The Town of the Queen of the Angels."

The Early Days

The people quickly built houses. On Olvera Street, they built a **plaza**. A plaza is a town square. There, people talked with their neighbors. They celebrated holidays together. The plaza felt just like home.

The small town grew quickly. It filled with many people. Some came from Mexico. Others came from different parts of the United States. People came from other countries, too. Los Angeles was a popular place to live.

The plaza was the center of the community.

The City Grows and Changes

Life in Los Angeles began to change. As the city got larger, new neighborhoods popped up. Families moved away from Olvera Street. They built new houses in other parts of town.

The plaza had been busy and joyful. Now it was quiet and sad. Buildings were ready to fall down. Olvera Street looked like a dirty alley. The smell of garbage filled the air. No one seemed to care about the old town of Los Angeles.

Soon, people forgot the old plaza. It was just a tiny part of a big city.

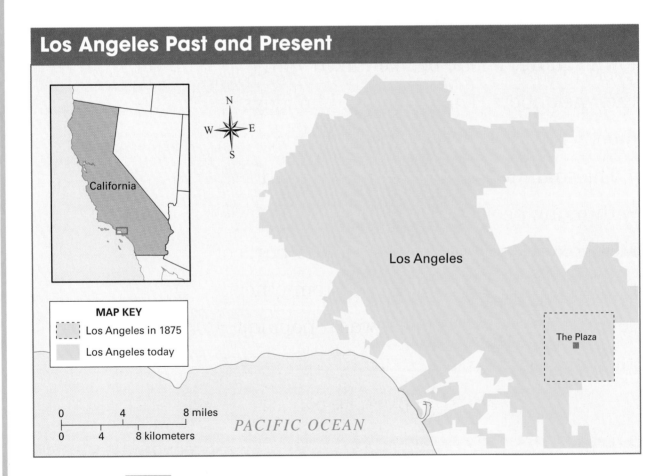

Los Angeles Past and Present

California

N
W E
S

MAP KEY
- - - Los Angeles in 1875
▓ Los Angeles today

Los Angeles

The Plaza

0   4   8 miles
0   4   8 kilometers

PACIFIC OCEAN

A Big, Busy City

The old plaza is full of life.

Los Angeles kept growing. Today, the city is spread over many miles. Homes, schools, and stores fill the neighborhoods. The city has railroads, highways, skyscrapers, hotels, museums, and parks. It also has crowded sidewalks and traffic.

What happened to old Los Angeles? The old plaza still stands. People raised money to fix the old buildings and markets there.

Now people visit the old part of town. They hear Mexican music there. They walk through the old houses. They dance in the plaza. Los Angeles has changed, but the plaza reminds people of how the city began.

10

How Did One Community Change?

You have learned that communities grow and change. As they do, they create history. History is what has happened in the past.

Now you will read how one community changed. San Francisco, California grew from a small town into a large city.

10.1 A Small Town

Long ago, many big ships sailed into San Francisco's harbor on the Pacific Ocean. A **harbor** is a place with deep water where ships can stop.

Many people on the ships decided to stay in San Francisco. They built houses, stores, and hotels.

Sailors on the ships needed goods from the town. People in the town needed goods from the ships. At the water's edge, people built docks where ships could unload goods.

This is how the town of San Francisco started to grow.

10.2 People Find Gold

In 1848, people found gold east of San Francisco. The word spread quickly around the world.

Many people traveled to San Francisco on their way to look for gold. They came from other parts of our country. They came from countries far away. They came in ships. They came on horses. They came in covered wagons.

Now there were many more people in San Francisco. They all needed places to eat and sleep. They needed lots of other things, too.

109

10.3 Becoming a City

People who look for gold are called gold miners. The miners needed food, clothing, and tents. They needed shovels to dig for gold. They needed pans to look for gold in streams. They found these things in San Francisco.

People opened new stores and businesses in San Francisco to help the miners. The miners kept coming. More people arrived to open more stores. They built more roads and houses, too. San Francisco grew into a small city.

10.4 Life in the City

Life in the city was not easy. People crowded the streets. There were long lines at stores. The streets were muddy and slippery.

San Francisco also faced a big danger— fire. Many new houses were built of wood. People used oil and gas lamps to see at night. These lamps caused fires easily. There were not enough firefighters to keep the city safe.

Still, San Francisco kept growing.

The earth shook.

The fires blazed.

Wednesday   Thursday   Friday

10.5 The San Francisco Earthquake

In 1906, San Francisco was a large city. Then, a terrible **earthquake** happened. An earthquake makes the ground shake.

Many buildings fell. Others caught on fire and burned. Firefighters could not save them all. Fires spread all over the city. The docks caught on fire, too. Many people lost their homes.

After the earthquake, many people lived in tents in the city parks. They were afraid to go near the rest of the buildings. They stood in long lines to get food and water.

After a while, people started to rebuild their homes and stores. Soon, San Francisco was growing again.

The docs are saved. **The city will rebuild.**

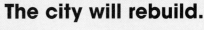

Saturday   Sunday

10.6 Timeline of the Earthquake

Timelines show when things happen. They can show things that happened over many years. They can show things that happened over less time, too.

Look at the timeline above. It tells the story of the San Francisco earthquake. Many people still think about this big event.

Summary

San Francisco grew from a small town into a big city. People built docks and buildings. Miners came to search for gold. More stores opened. In 1906, an earthquake and fires almost destroyed the city. Later, people built the city back up again.

Family Stories

All families have stories. Some tell what happened long ago. What can family stories tell us about how a city changed?

Many years ago, Rob Monaco and his father were in their basement. They were looking for old family photographs. Sure enough, Rob found some.

The two could not believe their eyes. A few boxes held hundreds of pictures. Rob's great-grandfather had taken them. They showed the history of San Francisco. Many showed the great earthquake of 1906.

J. B. Monaco was Rob's great-grandfather. He took pictures around San Francisco.

Rob and his father looked at the photographs. Rob's father pointed to one of a boy. "That is my father," he said. "His name was Dante Monaco."

Rob stared at the picture. In it Dante is sitting on a pile of bricks. He looks frightened. The photograph was taken a few days after the earthquake.

Rob thought about his own life in San Francisco. He felt very safe. "What was it like to live through the 1906 earthquake?" he wondered.

Dante was Rob's grandfather. He was about six years old in 1906.

115

Rob's father remembered hearing stories about the earthquake. "It hit the city early in the morning," he said. "Dante and his parents were asleep. Suddenly, the ground shook. Soon the city was on fire."

Dante's father, J. B. Monaco, helped his family get to safety. Then he took photographs of the city. He wanted to show what had happened.

J. B.'s pictures show heavy damage to San Francisco.

J. B. Monaco had taken many photographs of the city as it grew. After the earthquake, he took pictures that showed how the city changed.

Today, Rob is a grownup. He tells his own children stories about the earthquake. He shows them his great-grandfather's photographs of San Francisco. The stories and photographs are part of Rob's family history. They are part of San Francisco's history, too.

Rob and his children are part of San Francisco's history.

How Can One Person Make a Difference in a Community?

All communities have problems. They solve their problems in different ways. Sometimes one person thinks of a way to solve the problem. This makes the community a better place to live.

In this chapter, you will read about people who solved problems in their communities.

11.1 Jane Addams Gave Children a Place to Play

Jane Addams lived from 1860 to 1935. She lived in the city of Chicago, Illinois. She saw children playing in the dirty, crowded streets. She knew the children were not safe there.

Addams wanted to help. Soon she had an idea. She rented a building where children could play and be safe. She called it Hull House. Addams also built Chicago's first playground.

Jane Addams saw a problem in her community and solved it.

11.2 Garrett A. Morgan Made His Community Safer

Garrett A. Morgan lived from 1877 to 1963. He lived in Cleveland, Ohio. He was an inventor. An **inventor** thinks of new things, such as machines. An inventor often builds things, too.

Morgan thought the streets of his city were very crowded. Traffic lights had no delay between "Go" and "Stop." Cars often crashed into each other.

Morgan invented a traffic light that had three commands. Cars had time to slow down between "Go" and "Stop." Morgan's new traffic light helped keep the people of Cleveland safe.

11.3 Susan La Flesche Picotte Helped Sick People

Susan La Flesche Picotte (la FLESH pih-KAHT) lived from 1865 to 1915. She was an American Indian. She lived in the state of Nebraska. People in her community got sick from time to time. But often, there was no doctor to help them. This made young Susan sad.

Susan Picotte grew up and went away to school. She studied hard and became a doctor. She wanted to care for American Indians in her community.

Dr. Picotte rode a horse to visit her patients. Later, she started a hospital.

Dr. Picotte helped her community by caring for sick people.

11.4 Luis Valdez Helped Farmworkers

Luis Valdez was born in 1940. He lived in a community of farmworkers. He knew they worked hard. He knew they didn't have nice homes.

Valdez wrote plays about how hard their lives were. He took actors from farm to farm on trucks. They performed his plays in the fields. Many farmworkers saw his plays. So did other people. People learned about the farmworkers' struggles.

Luis Valdez helped people by teaching them. He taught farmworkers that they could have better lives. He taught other people that they could help the farmworkers.

Summary

All communities have problems to solve. Sometimes one person thinks of an idea to help make a community better.

Homework Help

Seeing a problem is the first step to solving it. An eighth grade girl named Jasmine saw children who needed help. How did she solve the problem in her community?

Jasmine wanted to help children with homework.

"Excuse me, Mrs. Dandridge. Can you help me with my homework?" a fifth grader asked as she came into the office of Mrs. Dandridge. Mrs. Dandridge works in Detroit, Michigan. She helps foster children and their families.

Jasmine Dandridge was in her mother's office. She had just finished her own homework after school. "I can help them," she thought. So, she did.

Jasmine thought about her mother's job. Every day children came into the office. Often, they asked Mrs. Dandridge for help with homework.

Jasmine was a Girl Scout. She thought about the Girl Scout Promise. Girl Scouts promise to try to help people at all times. Jasmine wanted to help the children with their homework.

First, she found out more about tutoring. (When you **tutor** people, you help them learn something.) She talked to teachers. She read books. She used the Internet. Then, she made a plan.

Jasmine learned ways she could help the children.

Jasmine put signs up around the office. Children started asking her for homework help. Soon she had a group of children. Jasmine worked with them for two hours, three days a week. First, she helped them with their homework. Then, she tutored them in reading, math, and spelling.

Jasmine's program was a success. The children learned how to study. They got better grades, too. One boy brought his math test to show Jasmine. At the top of the paper was a big A! He was so proud. So was Jasmine.

The homework club helped children learn.

The homework program was very popular. It grew bigger. Jasmine helped many children. She won the Girl Scout's Silver Award for her work.

Jasmine is proud of how she made a difference in her community. Helping people "is something that if you try it once, you will be hooked," she says. "You learn a lot from the people you provide services to. You also learn things about yourself."

Jasmine won an award for her hard work helping others.

127

How Do Leaders Help Their Communities?

Leaders are people who help make important decisions.

In this chapter, you will learn how people choose leaders. You will also learn what leaders do to help their communities.

12.1 People Vote for Leaders

In most communities, people vote for their leaders. When you **vote**, you say who you think is best.

People who want to be leaders tell the community their ideas. Then adults in the community vote for the person they think will be the best leader.

The **government** is the group of people chosen to lead a community. Leaders have many important jobs to do. It is hard work to be a leader. But it can be fun, too.

12.2 Leaders Help Make Laws

Community leaders help make laws for the community.

Some laws help people stay safe. There are laws to tell people how fast they should drive. There are laws to tell people where they can ride their bicycles and skateboards.

Some laws help the community stay clean and beautiful. There are laws to stop people from throwing trash on the ground. There are laws about where it is okay to walk a dog in a city.

12.3 Leaders Spend Money for Services

Community leaders decide how to spend the community's money.

Every community needs people to help keep it safe. This is the job of firefighters and police officers. Leaders decide how much money to spend on these services. They also decide how much to spend on fire trucks and police cars.

Every community needs people to work on its streets, sidewalks, and parks. Leaders decide how much money to pay these workers.

12.4 Leaders Decide What to Build

Community leaders decide where to build new buildings and parks.

Leaders think about what new buildings the community needs. They also think about what buildings will look like. They work with people in the community to make decisions. These decisions help make sure everyone can enjoy the buildings and parks in a community.

Summary

People vote for leaders to make important decisions. Leaders make laws for the community. They decide how to spend money on services. They decide what buildings and parks to build in the community.

Leaders Vote for the Dogs

Community leaders make many decisions. How do people work with leaders to make decisions for the community?

Wayne Resotka loves to play with his dog, Tucker. Tucker enjoys playing with other dogs and running free. But Wayne and Tucker live in Long Valley, New Jersey. Like many communities, Long Valley has laws about dogs. They are not allowed in any city parks.

Some people in Long Valley had backyards where their dogs could play. Others did not. Many dogs had no place to play with other dogs. They had no place to run free. Dog owners wanted to fix the problem.

Tucker loves to be outside.

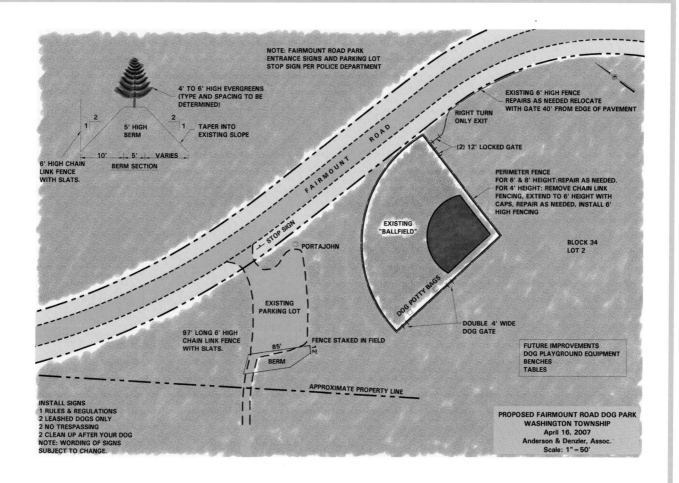

Within the image:

NOTE: FAIRMOUNT ROAD PARK
ENTRANCE SIGNS AND PARKING LOT
STOP SIGN PER POLICE DEPARTMENT

FAIRMOUNT ROAD

4' TO 6' HIGH EVERGREENS
(TYPE AND SPACING TO BE
DETERMINED)

5' HIGH
BERM

TAPER INTO
EXISTING SLOPE

6' HIGH CHAIN
LINK FENCE
WITH SLATS.

10'   5'   VARIES
BERM SECTION

EXISTING 6' HIGH FENCE
REPAIRS AS NEEDED. RELOCATE
WITH GATE 40' FROM EDGE OF PAVEMENT

RIGHT TURN
ONLY EXIT

(2) 12' LOCKED GATE

PERIMETER FENCE
FOR 6' & 8' HEIGHT:REPAIR AS NEEDED.
FOR 4' HEIGHT: REMOVE CHAIN LINK
FENCING, EXTEND TO 6' HEIGHT WITH
CAPS, REPAIR AS NEEDED. INSTALL 6'
HIGH FENCING

EXISTING
"BALLFIELD"

BLOCK 34
LOT 2

STOP SIGN

PORTAJOHN

DOG POTTY BAGS

EXISTING
PARKING LOT

97' LONG 6' HIGH
CHAIN LINK FENCE
WITH SLATS.

85'

BERM

FENCE STAKED IN FIELD

DOUBLE 4' WIDE
DOG GATE

FUTURE IMPROVEMENTS
DOG PLAYGROUND EQUIPMENT
BENCHES
TABLES

APPROXIMATE PROPERTY LINE

INSTALL SIGNS
1 RULES & REGULATIONS
2 LEASHED DOGS ONLY
2 NO TRESPASSING
2 CLEAN UP AFTER YOUR DOG
NOTE: WORDING OF SIGNS
SUBJECT TO CHANGE.

PROPOSED FAIRMOUNT ROAD DOG PARK
WASHINGTON TOWNSHIP
April 16, 2007
Anderson & Denzler, Assoc.
Scale: 1" = 50'

Wayne and some friends had an idea. No one used the ball field up on a hill. It would make a perfect dog park, where dogs could play without leashes.

Wayne formed a group to work on the project. First he asked people's opinions. Many people said they would like a dog park and would help build it.

Wayne went to the town hall. He told the town leaders why dog owners wanted the park. He said that dog owners would pay for the dog park and take care of it.

Town leaders studied plans for the dog park.

Not everyone was happy about the idea. There is a horse farm near the ball field. The farm's owner was afraid the dogs would scare her horses. Other people worried the dog park could cost the town a lot of money. They shared their fears with the town leaders.

Town leaders asked a lot of questions. They listened to both sides. Then they took a vote. They decided the dog park would be good for Long Valley. They told Wayne his group could build the park.

Volunteers got to work. People raised money to buy fences. They cleaned up the fields and planted new grass.

At the town hall, town leaders voted "yes" for the dog park.

Kids helped, too. Emily Peel wanted to build a path. She showed her plans to the town leaders. They liked her idea. Emily pulled weeds, moved rocks, and poured gravel for her path.

Justin Guenther also helped. He built a picnic area. He also made a flower garden.

Now dogs and owners love the dog park. It's a great example of how people worked with town leaders to make good decisions for the community.

Emily worked hard on the path.

Long Valley dogs enjoy their park.

What Does a Good Citizen Do?

Many people work hard to make their community a good place to live. You have learned how community leaders help. Now you will learn how citizens help.

A **citizen** is an official member of a community. Some citizens are born in the community. Others move to the community.

13.1 Communities Need Good Citizens

Good citizens work to make their communities better.

Grown-up citizens vote for community leaders. They obey the laws. They help keep their communities clean and safe.

Children cannot vote in the community. But they can be good citizens. They can obey the laws. They can help make their communities better.

13.2 Good Citizens Get Along with Others

Good citizens of all ages try to get along.

They work together. They listen to what other people say. They solve problems by talking about different ideas. If a problem is serious, good citizens know how to ask for help.

Good citizens care about people in their community. They don't tease or call people names. They are kind to others.

13.3 Good Citizens Help Others

Good citizens find ways to help others. Here are some ideas.

Good citizens collect food and clothes for people who need them. They visit friends who are sick. They call people who are lonely.

Good citizens make decorations for a hospital. They visit people in nursing homes. They send cards to people who are sad.

Good citizens carry packages for older people. They help neighbors clean up a yard. They help children with projects.

What other ways can you think of to help people?

13.4 Good Citizens Help Care for Their Community

Good citizens care about their community. They want it to look nice. They do many things to keep their community pretty.

Good citizens take care of their homes. They also take care of places that everyone shares. They throw trash away, not on the ground. They help plant community gardens.

Good citizens can recycle cans, bottles, and paper. They can plant trees and flowers for everyone to enjoy.

Summary

Good citizens work to make their community a better place. They get along with others. They find ways to help others. They help care for their community.

Good Citizen Lincoln

Abraham Lincoln had a hard childhood. He worked to help his family. He could not go to school much. How did this regular citizen become our president?

Abraham Lincoln was born about 200 years ago. He was born in Kentucky. His family was very poor. His mother died when he was only 9 years old.

Lincoln helped run the family farm. The work was hard, but he was strong. He cut down trees and built fences. Sometimes he worked for other farmers. Lincoln gave the money he earned to his father.

Lincoln went to school only once in a while. Still, he learned to read and write. He loved to learn.

Lincoln was famous for how much wood he could split in a day.

Lincoln was a popular speaker.

As a young man, Lincoln tried different jobs. He sailed a boat down the Mississippi River. He delivered mail. He worked in a store. Everywhere he went, Lincoln talked to people. He listened to their problems.

Lincoln settled in Illinois. He became a lawyer. Voters elected him to the state legislature. A **legislature** is a group of elected leaders who make laws. People respected him. Some people called him "Honest Abe."

In the 1850s, Lincoln grew worried. The country was in trouble. Some states had **slavery**. Slavery meant people could own other people. Some states did not have slavery. People feared the states would fight about slavery.

Lincoln believed slavery was wrong. He wanted to help the country solve this problem. He wanted to help people learn to treat everyone the same way. So, he ran for president of the United States in 1860.

Many people died in the Civil War.

Granger Collection, NY

Lincoln won the election. The states with slavery were angry. They did not want to be part of the country any more. President Lincoln said the states could not leave. He said the United States must stay together.

States from the north fought states from the south in the Civil War. Many people died. Many towns were ruined. It was the worst war ever fought in our country.

President Lincoln was a strong leader. He led the states from the north to victory. He kept the nation together. Before the war was over, Lincoln ended slavery.

Today, people remember Abraham Lincoln as a great leader. They remember the young boy who worked hard and loved to learn. They celebrate Lincoln's life as a good citizen.

IN THIS TEMPLE
AS IN THE HEARTS OF THE PEOPLE
FOR WHOM HE SAVED THE UNION
THE MEMORY OF ABRAHAM LINCOLN
IS ENSHRINED FOREVER

This statue honors Abraham Lincoln.

What Do Communities Share?

The United States of America is our country. It is made up of 50 states. Each state has many different communities.

Communities in our country share many things. In this chapter, you will learn how communities share. You will learn how they help each other.

14.1 We Are Many Communities

In our country, some communities are big and some are small. Some are rural. Some are urban. And some are suburban.

Communities have different geography. Some have deserts. Some are near the ocean. Some are in the mountains or on the plains.

No community in our country has everything it needs to live. Communities share what they have.

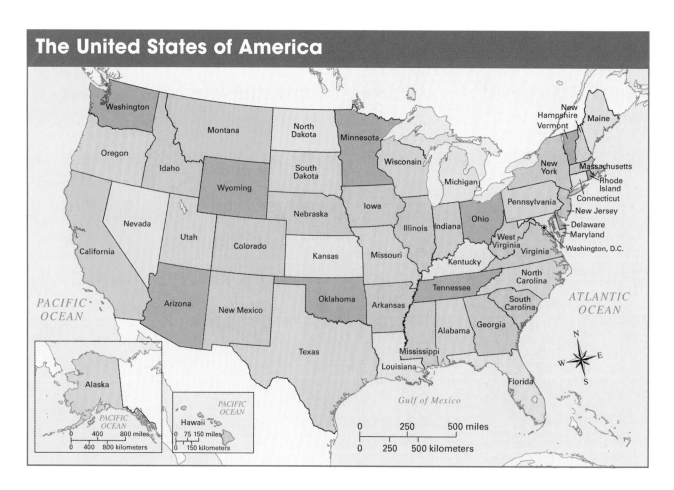

The United States of America

14.2 Communities Share Their Food

Food comes from many different places in our country. Fish comes from oceans, rivers, and lakes. Communities near these places share their fish with others. Beef comes from communities with lots of grass for cows to eat. Communities on the plains grow wheat and corn. Fruit comes from communities with warm weather.

People move food from where it is produced to where others need it.

Where do you think your favorite food comes from?

14.3 Communities Share Their Goods

Many of the things you use were made in other communities.

Your family car might have come from Michigan. Your school's computers might have come from California.

No community can make everything it needs and wants. We get goods from other communities. They may get goods from our community.

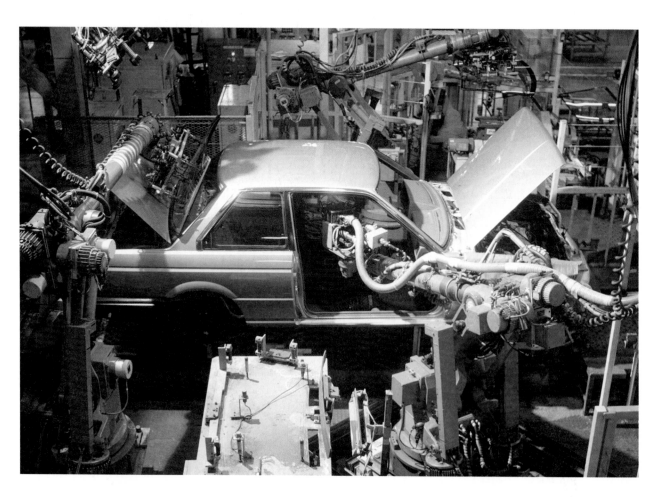

14.4 Communities Share Their Special Places

Every community has special places. Some communities have pretty beaches. Some have big cities. Others have quiet forests.

People who travel to other communities are called **tourists**. They go to see new places. They also go to meet new people.

Which communities in our country have you visited?

14.5 Communities Share Happy and Sad Times

People in communities like to share their happy times. They have festivals, parades, and games. They invite people from far away to enjoy these events with them.

Communities have sad times, too. A flood, tornado, or earthquake might hit a community. Then the community asks others for help. People all over the country send food, clothing, and money to help those in need.

14.6 Communities Share Their Pride

People in communities share their pride in our country. They fly the American flag. They say the Pledge of Allegiance to the flag. They sing songs about our country and our history. They care for our historic buildings, statues, and parks.

How do you show your pride in the United States?

Summary

Communities share things people need and want. Some share food. Others share goods. Many share their special places. They share happy times. They help each other in sad times. People in communities share their pride in our country.

Happy Birthday, USA!

The communities in our country share many things. We share a birthday, too. July 4th is our country's birthday. How does the community of Philadelphia celebrate this important day?

Bong . . . bong . . . bong.

It is the Fourth of July. In Philadelphia, Pennsylvania, six young people stand by the Liberty Bell. The bell is too old and cracked to ring now. So they tap it gently 13 times. That's because this bell rang out 13 times on July 4, 1776. That day was our country's birthday.

Every year, communities across the United States ring their bells on this special day. They ring each bell 13 times. This is one way to say "Happy Birthday" to our country.

Visitors can touch the Liberty Bell.

Before 1776, our country did not exist. Instead, there were 13 colonies. A **colony** is an area run by another country. The American colonies were run by Great Britain.

This painting shows the signing of the Declaration of Independence.

In July 1776, some leaders in the colonies changed things. They signed a paper called the Declaration of Independence. It said the colonies were free states. It said the states did not need Great Britain. The states could run themselves. These new states formed the United States of America.

Actors read the Declaration every July in Philadelphia.

Brave leaders from every colony signed the Declaration. They had not liked many of Great Britain's laws. They wanted their own government. Signing the Declaration could make the war with Great Britain much worse. They risked their lives to help create our country.

One of these men was Thomas Jefferson. He led the group that wrote the Declaration. He wrote that all people are equal. Each of us has the right to live and have **freedom**. Freedom means being free to choose how you act. Each of us has the right to make a good life.

All Americans share those rights. On July 4th, we celebrate the birth of our free country and our freedom.

People in Philadelphia are proud of their community. It has a great history. The Declaration was signed there. It is where the U.S. Constitution was written. The Constitution set up the government of the new country.

Philadelphia says "Happy Birthday, USA!" in a big way. They have a parade. There is a concert. At night, the city has a huge fireworks show. Thousands of people come to the city to celebrate.

Across our country, we all say "Happy Birthday, USA!" on July 4th. We celebrate the freedom that we enjoy each day.

Fireworks light up the sky on July 4th.

Landmarks of Citizenship

Special Days, Special Places

Washington, D.C.: Everybody's City

The United States has many special celebrations and places. Let's take a trip to learn more. At each stop, we can learn about the history of our country.

Our first stop is Washington, D.C. This city is the capital of the United States. It was named for our first president. He was George Washington.

Washington, D.C. is the center of our government. The president lives and works in the White House. Congress makes laws in the Capitol. The Supreme Court is the highest court in the land.

About 25 million people vist Washington, D.C. each year.

In Washington, D.C. we can see the Declaration of Independence. Our nation began with this document on July 4, 1776. So, we celebrate July 4 every year. We call it Independence Day.

We can see the Constitution in Washington, D.C., too. The Constitution sets up our nation's government. We live by its rules.

The Bill of Rights is part of the Constitution. It protects the rights of all Americans. One important right is the freedom of speech.

Our country's most important documents are kept together in one room.

New York City: Welcome to the United States

When you come to New York City by ship, the Statue of Liberty welcomes you. She stands on an island in the harbor. Her name tells you that the United States is a land of freedom.

In the past, many immigrants came here from Europe. (Immigrants are people who move to a new country.) They sailed past the Statue of Liberty. They stopped at Ellis Island, nearby. There, they entered the United States. This was their first step toward becoming U.S. citizens.

Today, many people visit the Statue of Liberty. They visit the museum on Ellis Island, too.

Old Glory, Our Flag

The American flag is a symbol of our country. The 13 stripes stand for the first 13 states. The 50 stars mean there are 50 states today.

We pledge allegiance to the flag. That means we promise to honor the flag and our country.

We sing about the flag, too. Our national song is "The Star Spangled Banner." It calls our country "the land of the free and the home of the brave."

June 14 is Flag Day. On this day we remember when "the stars and stripes" became our national flag.

East 42nd St

Giving Thanks in Plymouth

Plimoth Plantation, in Plymouth, Massachusetts, is a great place to visit. It is a living museum. People there dress as they would have in 1627. They speak and act as people did then, too.

On Thanksgiving Day, museum workers remember a special event. In 1621, the Pilgrims and the Wampanoag Indians held a feast to give thanks. The Pilgrims had come from England a year before. The Wampanoags helped the Pilgrims hunt and grow food.

At the feast, people probably ate pumpkin and turkey or duck. They gave thanks for a good harvest.

Now, Thanksgiving Day is a holiday in the United States. It is on the fourth Thursday in November. Many people cook a turkey feast. Some Americans thought the turkey should be our national bird. But instead, we chose the bald eagle.

On Thanksgiving Day, some people visit Plymouth. All over the country, people give thanks. We remember how the Pilgrims and the Wampanoags joined together in 1621. We join with our own family and friends. We remember all that we are thankful for.

Americans celebrate Thanksgiving in November. On this day, we give thanks.

Honoring the Presidents at Mount Rushmore

Look up at the side of the mountain. There are four huge faces carved in stone. Each one is about 60 feet high!

This is Mount Rushmore in South Dakota. The stone faces are four presidents.

Our first president, George Washington, is there. He led us to independence.

Thomas Jefferson is next to him. He wrote the Declaration of Independence.

Next is Theodore Roosevelt. He led the nation to become a world power.

Abraham Lincoln is on the right. He kept our country together during the Civil War.

On the third Monday in February, we honor all our presidents. That special holiday is President's Day.

An artist spent six and a half years carving the faces.

Mount Rushmore is one of many beautiful places in our nation. There many ways to show we are proud of our land.

Some people like to sing "America the Beautiful." It is one of our special songs. It celebrates the beauty of the United States "from sea to shining sea."

Painters celebrate our nation's beauty, too. This painting shows the Rocky Mountains. A painting lets us all see "America the beautiful."

Albert Bierstadt made paintings of the West. Here are the Rocky Mountains.

Memorial Day in Toledo

We are in Toledo, Ohio, on the last Monday in May. This is Memorial Day. People visit the cemeteries here. In all, they place more than 5,000 American flags on veteran's graves. (Veterans are people who served in the armed forces.)

Across the nation, people honor those who have died in wars. Many communities have parades. Toledo has two parades. Bands play. Veterans march. People wave and clap.

People also give speeches about those who have died for our country.

People across the country honor and thank veterans with flags and parades.

This memorial in Washington, D.C. honors veterans of the Vietnam War.

Veteran's Day in Texas

Here we are in McAllen, Texas. It is November 11, Veterans Day. Many people visit the Veterans War Memorial of Texas. They honor the soldiers who serve us today. They remember those who have died, too.

In Austin, Texas, a big Veterans Day parade starts at 9 o'clock. Scouts and veterans march. Bands play our country's special songs. People wave American flags. They show that they are proud of the men and women in our armed forces.

All veterans have helped protect our freedom.

Working Together in San Francisco

Now we are in San Francisco, California, on the first Monday in September. We can see crowds of people enjoying events in the city. Like most people in the United States, these people have the day off from work. The day is Labor Day.

People relax and have fun on Labor Day.

Labor Day has been a holiday in the United States for more than 100 years. It is a day for workers to relax. Many people in San Francisco go to concerts, picnics, or plays. They take boat trips on San Francisco Bay. Across the country, people spend time with their families and friends.

These immigrant children entered the country through Angel Island.

Labor Day is a holiday to honor all workers.

Many workers came here from Asia. Most of them entered the United States through San Francisco Bay.

Angel Island is in the bay. Today it is a state park. But for many years, it was like Ellis Island, It was a place where immigrants entered this country.

About 1 million people from Asia passed through Angel Island. Many of them helped build California's cities. They worked on our country's railroads, too.

On Labor Day we say thank you to everyone who helps our country.

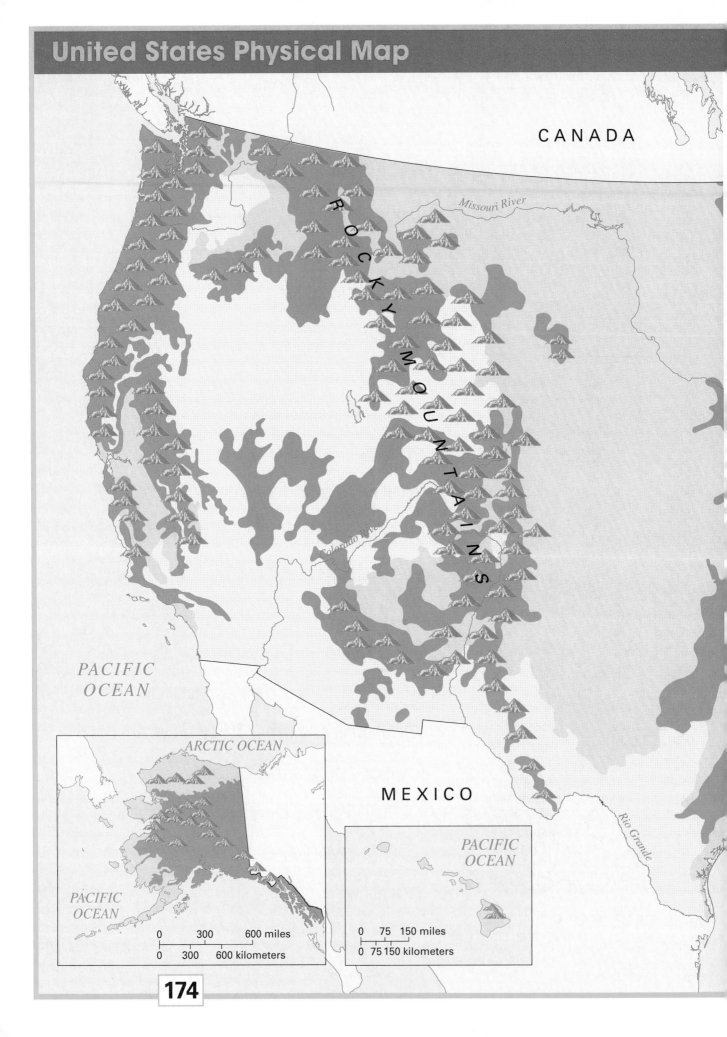

CANADA

Missouri River

R
O
C
K
Y

M
O
U
N
T
A
I
N
S

Colorado River

PACIFIC
OCEAN

ARCTIC OCEAN

MEXICO

PACIFIC
OCEAN

PACIFIC
OCEAN

Rio Grande

0	300	600 miles
0	300	600 kilometers

0	75	150 miles
0	75	150 kilometers

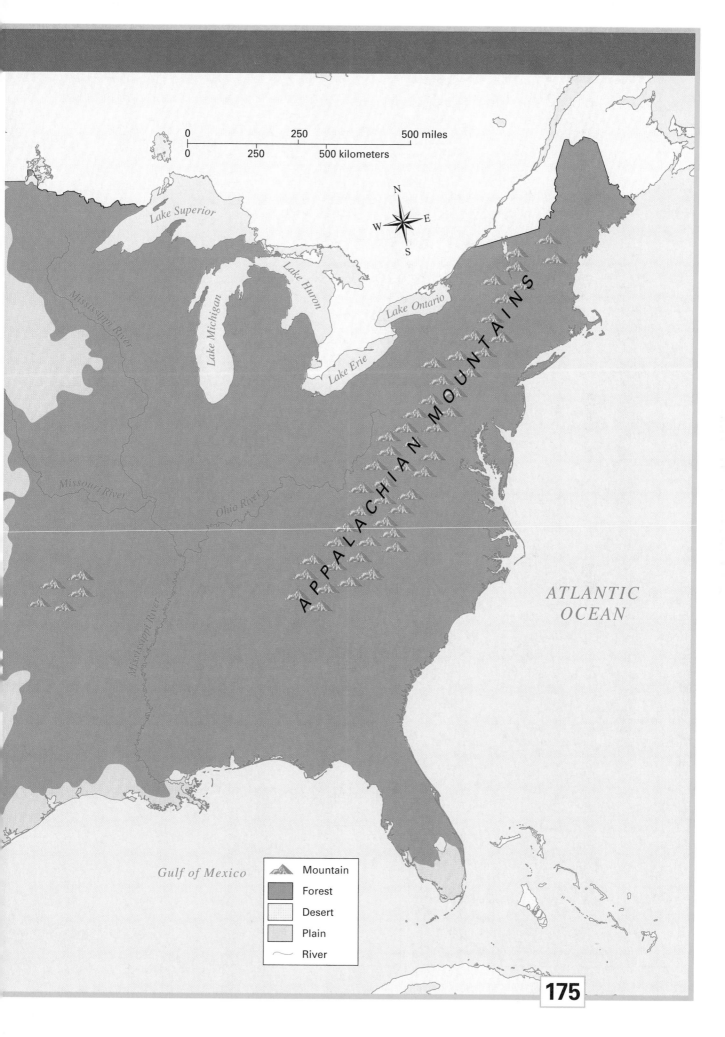

Lake Superior

Lake Michigan

Lake Huron

Lake Ontario

Lake Erie

Mississippi River

Missouri River

Ohio River

Mississippi River

APPALACHIAN MOUNTAINS

ATLANTIC
OCEAN

Gulf of Mexico

0   250   500 miles

0   250   500 kilometers

N
W E
S

Mountain
Forest
Desert
Plain
River

United States Political Map

CANADA

Washington
★ Olympia

★ Salem

Oregon

★ Boise
Idaho

★ Helena
Montana

North Dakota
Bismarck ★

South Dakota
Pierre ★

Wyoming

Cheyenne ★

Nebraska

Lincoln

Sacramento ★

★ Carson City
Nevada

★ Salt Lake City
Utah

★ Denver
Colorado

Kansas

California

★ Santa Fe

Arizona
★ Phoenix

New Mexico

Oklahoma City ★
Oklahoma

PACIFIC OCEAN

Texas

ARCTIC OCEAN

MEXICO

Austin ★

Alaska

PACIFIC OCEAN

Juneau ★

| 0 | 300 | 600 miles |
| 0 | 300 | 600 kilometers |

PACIFIC OCEAN
Honolulu ★

Hawaii

| 0 | 75 | 150 miles |
| 0 | 75 | 150 kilometers |

176

0   250   500 miles
0   250   500 kilometers

New Hampshire

Maine

★ Augusta

Vermont

★ Montpelier

★ Concord

Boston

Albany ★

Massachusetts ★ Providence

New York

Hartford ★

Rhode Island

Connecticut

Minnesota

St. Paul ★

Wisconsin

★ Madison

Michigan

★ Lansing

Pennsylvania

★ Harrisburg

★ Trenton

New Jersey

Iowa

★ Des Moines

Illinois

Indiana

★ Indianapolis

Ohio

★ Columbus

Annapolis ★ Dover

Washington, D.C.

Delaware

Maryland

West Virginia

★ Charleston

Virginia

★ Richmond

Topeka ★

Jefferson City ★

Missouri

Springfield ★

Kentucky

★ Frankfort

North Carolina

★ Raleigh

ATLANTIC OCEAN

Nashville ★

Tennessee

Arkansas

Little Rock ★

South Carolina

★ Columbia

Atlanta ★

Mississippi

Alabama

Georgia

Louisiana

★ Jackson

Montgomery ★

Baton Rouge ★

★ Tallahassee

Florida

Gulf of Mexico

U.S. capital

★ State capital

177

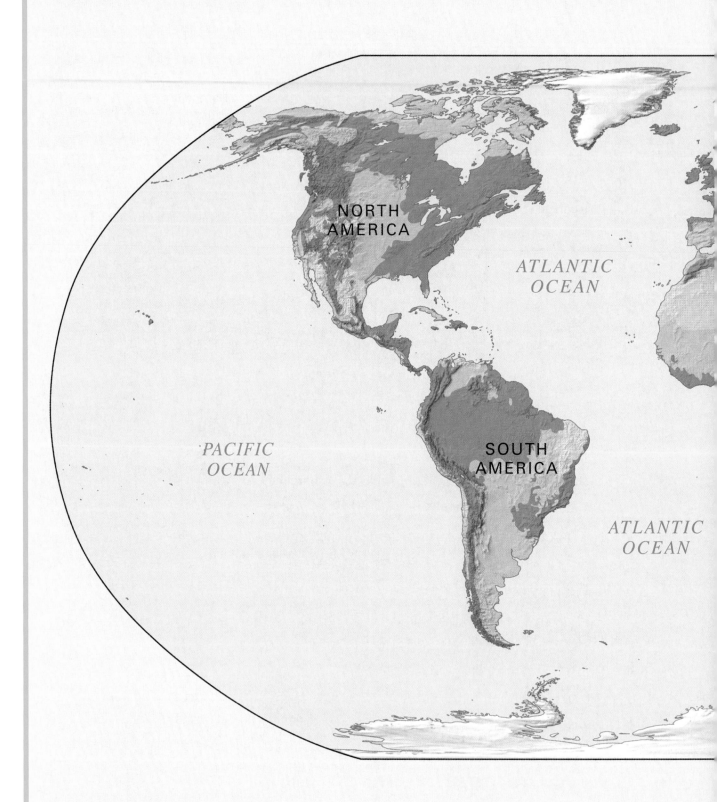

NORTH
AMERICA

*ATLANTIC
OCEAN*

*PACIFIC
OCEAN*

SOUTH
AMERICA

*ATLANTIC
OCEAN*

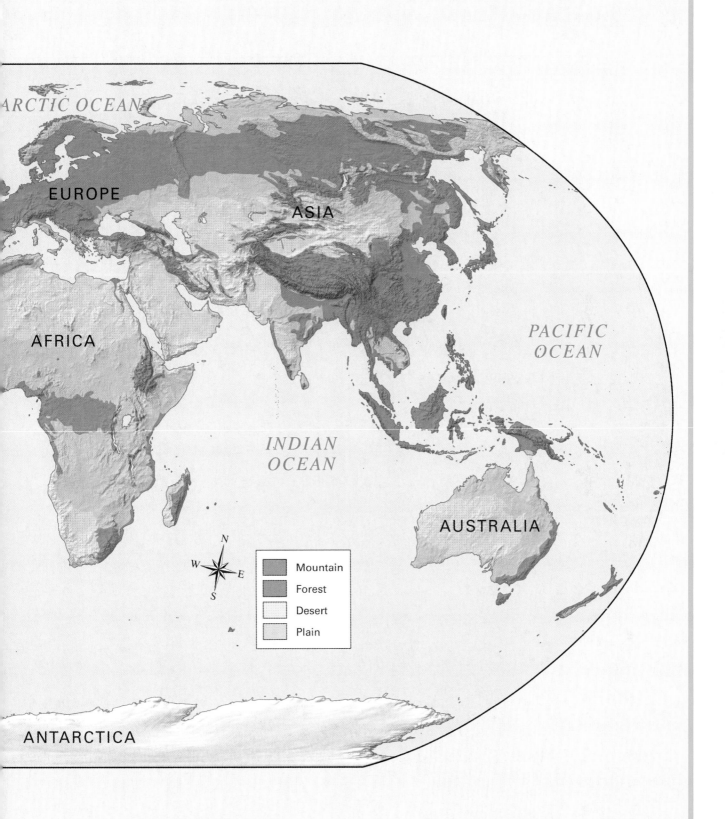

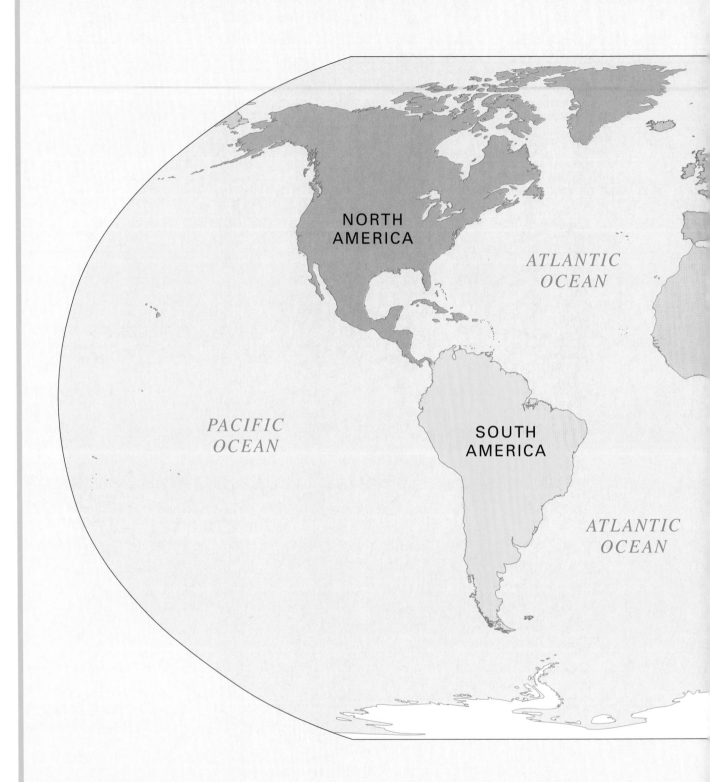

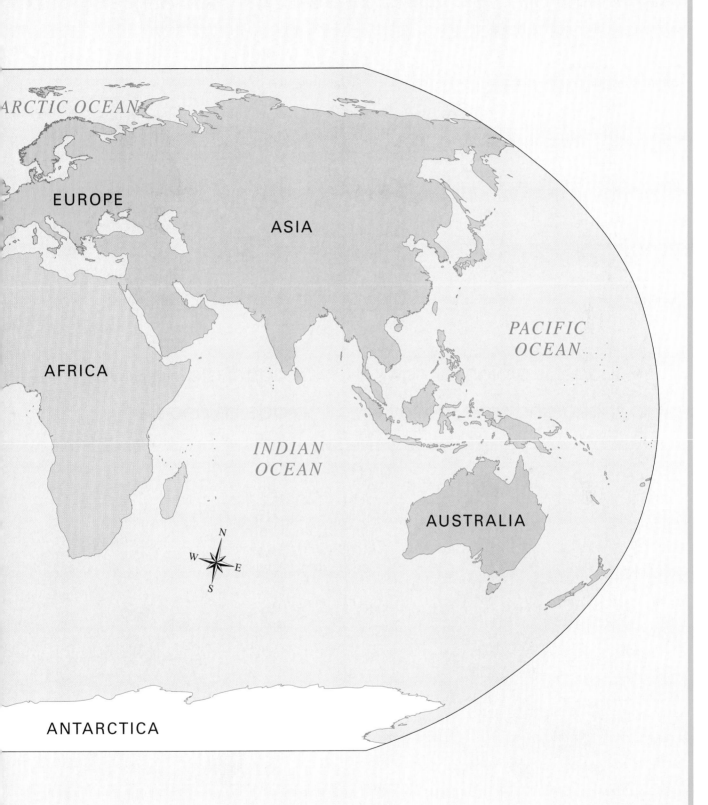

ARCTIC OCEAN

EUROPE

ASIA

PACIFIC
OCEAN

AFRICA

INDIAN
OCEAN

AUSTRALIA

N
W   E
S

ANTARCTICA

budget

A budget is a plan for how to spend and save money.

canal

A canal is a waterway made by people.

citizen

A citizen is an official member of a community.

colony

Great Britain's North American Colonies

A colony is a community ruled by a different country than it is in.

community

A community is a place where people live, work, play, and solve problems together.

compass

A compass shows direction.

compass rose

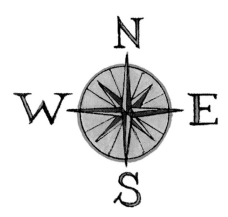

A compass rose shows directions on a map.

continent

North America

Continents are the seven large bodies of land on Earth.

desert

A desert is land that is hot and dry.

earthquake

An earthquake makes the ground shake.

environment

Everything around us is our environment.

freedom

Freedom is being free to choose how you act.

geography

Geography is the study of Earth's land, water, and people.

goods

Goods are things that can be bought, sold, and traded.

government

A government is the group of people chosen to lead a community.

harbor

A harbor is a place with deep water, where ships can stop.

inventor

An inventor creates new things.

island

An island is land with water all around it.

lake

A lake is a body of water with land all around it.

law

A law is a rule that tells people what they can and cannot do.

leader

A leader is a person who helps make important decisions.

legislature

The legislature is the group of leaders who make laws for a community.

map grid

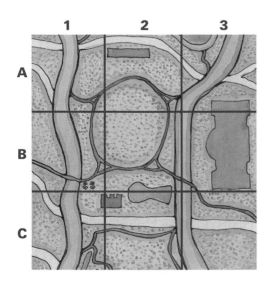

A map grid is a set of lines that help us find places on a map.

map key

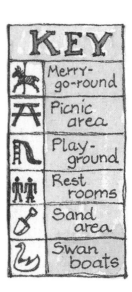

A map key tells what the symbols on a map mean.

map scale

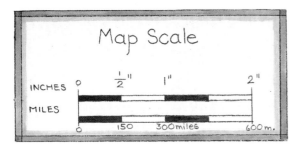

A map scale explains distance on a map.

mountain

Mountains are the tallest kind of land on Earth.

natural resource

Natural resources are things in nature that people use.

need

A need is something you must have to live.

ocean

Oceans are the largest bodies of water on Earth.

plain

Plains are large areas of flat land, usually covered in grass.

plaza

A plaza is an open area where people in a community come together.

pollute

To pollute is to hurt the environment.

river

A river is a body of fresh water that moves through land.

rural

Rural communities are small towns and farms that are far from cities.

save

You save money when you put it away and do not spend it.

service

Jobs in which people help other people are services.

slavery

In slavery, one person owns another person.

suburb

A suburb is a community just outside of a city.

suburban

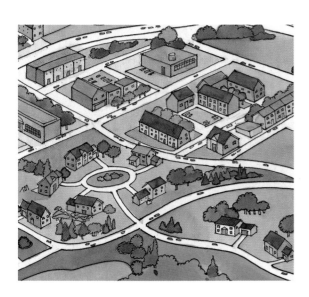

A community just outside of a city is a suburban community.

symbol

A symbol is a picture or color that stands for something on a map.

timeline

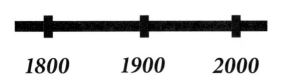

1800   1900   2000

A timeline shows when things happen.

tourist

A tourist is someone who travels to another community to enjoy it.

transportation

Transportation is how things are moved from place to place.

tutor

When you help people learn something, you tutor them.

urban

A community with lots of buildings and people is an urban community.

valley

A valley is a low place between mountains.

vote

When you vote, you say who you think should get something.

want

A want is something you would like to have but don't need to live.

193

Photographs

Cover

Elie Bernager/Getty Images

Chapter 1

4: Steve Dunwell/Index Stock **5**: Walter Hodges/Getty Images **6**: Hutchings Stock Photography/Digital Light Source **7**: Corbis Royalty Free **8-11**: Ron Munden/Munden Expressions

Chapter 2

14: Digital Stock/Corbis **15**: Richard T. Nowitz/Corbis **16**: Dewitt Jones/Corbis **17**: Photodisc/Getty Images **18**: David Frazier/Corbis **19**: Photodisc/Getty Images **20**: SuperStock, Inc./SuperStock **21**: Time & Life Pictures/Getty Images **22**: Library of Congress **23**: Richard Hutchings/Digital Light Source

Chapter 3

26 TL: AirPhotoUSA **27 BL**: David Frazier/Corbis

Chapter 4

38 BL: Angelo Cavalli/Getty Images **38 T**: Charles Smith/Corbis **39 TR**: Hisham Ibrahim/Getty Images **39 B**: David Frazier/Corbis **40 TL**: Photodisc/Getty Images **40 B**: Barry Howe/Corbis **41 T**: Photodisc/Getty Images **41 BR**: Frans Lemmens/Getty Images **44**: Photo Courtesy of Bill Bradlee & David Kroodsma/www.rideforclimate.com **45 T**: Photo Courtesy of Bill Bradlee & David Kroodsma/www.rideforclimate.com **45 BR**: Photo Courtesy of Bill Bradlee & David Kroodsma/www.rideforclimate.com **47**: Photo Courtesy of Bill Bradlee & David Kroodsma/www.rideforclimate.com

Chapter 5

50: David Frazier/Corbis **51 BL**: Photodisc/Getty Images **51 BR**: Photodisc/Getty Images **52 Inset**: David Toase/Getty Images **52 T**: James Gritz/Getty Images **53 T**: Barbara Peacock/Getty Images **53 B**: Photodisc/Getty Images **54 T**: Photodisc/Getty Images **54 B**: Jan Butchofsky-Houser/Corbis **55**: David Woodfall/Getty Images **56**: Tracy Montana/PhotoLink/Getty Images **57**: David Frazier/Corbis **58**: SuperStock, Inc./SuperStock **61**: Bettman/Corbis

Chapter 6

64: Photodisc/Getty Images **65**: Reuters/Corbis **66**: Owen Franken/Corbis **67**: David Frazier/Getty Images **68**: Mahaux Photography/Getty Images **69**: Richard Ransier/Corbis **70**: Jim Wark/Airphoto **71**: Christopher T. Frank California Stock Photo/Digital Railroad **73 TL**: Bob Daemmrich/PhotoEdit **73 TM**: Comstock/Jupiter Images **73 TR**: Felicia Martinez/PhotoEdit **74**: Jimmy Dorantes/Latin Focus

Chapter 7

78: Eyewire/Getty Images **79**: Jose Luis Pelaez/Corbis **80**: Masterfile Royalty Free **81**: Creatas/Superstock **82**: Michael Yamashita/Corbis **83**: Sandra Baker/Alamy **84**: AP Photo/Jennifer Szymaszek **85**: AP Photo/Diane Bondareff

Chapter 8

88: Lee White/Corbis **89**: Ryan McVay/Getty Images **90**: SW Productions/Getty Images **91**: David Young-Wolff/PhotoEdit

Chapter 9

98: Yellow Dog Productions/Getty Images
99: Lake County Museum/Corbis **100**: Arthur Rothstein/Corbis **101**: Charles E. Rotkin/Corbis **102**: Granger Collection, NY **103**: SPNB/Los Angeles Public Library **105**: David Young-Wolff/PhotoEdit

Chapter 10

108: Corbis **109**: Library of Congress **110**: San Francisco Library **111**: San Francisco Library **112 L**: Corbis **112 R**: A.L Murat/Corbis **113 L**: Corbis **113 R**: San Fransisco Library **114**: Photo Courtesy of the Monaco Family **115**: Photo Courtesy of the Monaco Family **116**: Photo Courtesy of the Monaco Family **117**: Photo Courtesy of the Monaco Family

Chapter 11

120: University Archives, The University Library, The University of Illinois at Chicago **121**: The Western Reserve Historical Society Library, Cleveland, Ohio **122**: MCP Hahnemann University - Archives and Special Collections on Women in Medicine **123**: Courtesy El Teatro Campesino, San Juan Bautista, California **124**: Photo Courtesy of Girl Scouts of Metro Detroit

Chapter 12

130: Shelley Gazin/Corbis **131 BL**: Kent Knudson/PhotoLink/Getty Images **131 BM**: Tim/Teacher's Curriculum Institute **131 BR**: Kent Knudson/PhotoLink/Getty Images **132 T**: Roger Wood/Corbis **132 B**: MI Harris/Getty Images **134**: Photo Courtesy of Wayne Rosotka **135**: Photo Courtesy of Wayne Rosotka **136**: Photo Courtesy of Wayne Rosotka **137**: Photo Courtesy of James Peel **137 B**: Photo Courtesy of Wayne Resotka

Chapter 13

140: Photo Courtesy of Christy Uyeno **141**: Terry Vine/Getty Images **142**: SW Productions/Getty Images **143**: Jose Luis Pelaez, Inc./Corbis **144**: North Wind/North Wind Picture Archives **145**: Bettman/Corbis **146**: Granger Collection, NY **147**: iStockphoto.com

Chapter 14

151: Mark Segal/Getty Images **152**: Kim Steele/Getty Images **153**: Jack Hollingsworth/Corbis **154**: VisionsofAmerica/Joe Sohm/Getty Images **155**: Michael Newman/PhotoEdit **156**: Leif Skoogfors/Corbis **157**: Granger Collection, NYC **158**: National Park Service, Independence National Historical Park **159**: Associated Press

Glossary

160 background: Prisma/SuperStock **160 foreground**: Ariel Skelley/Corbis **161 foreground**: Ariel Skelley/Corbis **162 BL**: David Noble Photography/Alamy **162 BR**: Rob Crandall/Alamy **163 BR**: Tetra Images/Corbis **163 BL**: Michael Ventura/Alamy **164**: Prisma/SuperStock **165**: Erick Nguyen/Alamy **166**: Bettmann/Corbis **167**: Paul Barton/Corbis **168 T**: AGE Fotostock/Superstock **169 B**: "Sunset in the Rockies (oil on canvas), Bierstadt, Albert (1830-1902)/Private Collection, Photo ©Christie's Images/The Bridgeman Art Library International" **170**: Associated Press **171**: Will & Deni McIntyre/Getty Images **172 T**: JupiterImages/ Brand X/Alamy **173 B**: Bettmann/Corbis **184 TR**: Corbis **185 BR**: Corbis **191 TL**: Corbis **191 TR**: RF/Corbis

Art

Table of Contents

1 T: Renate Lohmann **1 C**: Len Ebert **1 B**: Renate Lohmann **2 T**: Rosiland Solomon **2 C**: Siri Weber Feeney **2 B**: Doug Roy **3 T**: Len Ebert **3 C**: Jane McCreary **3 B**: Doug Roy **4 T**: Rosiland Solomon **4 C**: Len Ebert **4 B**: Carol Newsome **5 T**: Susan Jaekel **5 C**: Doug Roy

Chapter 1

2-3: Renate Lohmann

Chapter 2

12-13: Len Ebert

Chapter 3

24-25: Renate Lohmann **26**: Renate Lohmann **27**: Renate Lohmann **28**: Renate Lohmann **29**: Renate Lohmann **30**: Susan Jaekel **31**: Susan Jaekel **32**: Susan Jaekel **33**: Susan Jaekel **34**: Susan Jaekel **35**: Susan Jaekel

Chapter 4

36-37: Rosiland Solomon **43**: Susan Jaekel

Chapter 5

48-49: Siri Weber Feeney **60**: Len Ebert

Chapter 6

62-63: Doug Roy **75**: Len Ebert

Chapter 7

76-77: Len Ebert

Chapter 8

86-87: Jane McCreary **92**: Susan Jaekel **93**: Susan Jaekel **94**: Susan Jaekel **95**: Susan Jaekel

Chapter 9

96-97: Doug Roy

Chapter 10

106-107: Rosiland Solomon

Chapter 11

118-119: Len Ebert **124**: Siri Weber Feeney **125**: Siri Weber Feeney **126**: Siri Weber Feeney **127**: Siri Weber Feeney

Chapter 12

128-129: Carol Newsome

Chapter 13

138-139: Susan Jaekel

Chapter 14

148-149: Doug Roy

Glossary

149 TL: Susan Jaekel **149 TR**: Doug Roy **149 BL**: Susan Jaekel **149 BR**: Len Ebert **150 TL**: Len Ebert **150 TR**: Len Ebert **150 BL**: Renate Lohmann **150 BR**: Len Ebert **151 TL**: Doug Roy **151 BL**: Doug Roy **151 BR**: Doug Roy **152 TR**: Doug Roy **152 BL**: Carol Newsome **153 TL**: Len Ebert **153 TR**: Doug Roy **153 BL**: Doug Roy **153 BR**: Doug Roy **154 TL**: Carol Newsome **154 TR**: Susan Jaekel **154 BL**: Renate Lohmann **154 BR**: Renate Lohmann **155 TL**: Susan Jaekel **155 TR**: Doug Roy **155 BL**: Doug Roy **155 BR**: Doug Roy **156 TL**: Doug Roy **156 TR**: Doug Roy **156 BL**: Susan Jaekel **156 BR**: Susan Jaekel **157 TL**: Doug Roy **157 TR**: Len Ebert **157 BL**: Doug Roy **157 BR**: Len Ebert **159 TR**: Susan Jaekel **159 BL**: Len Ebert **159 BR**: Siri Weber Feeney **160 TL**: Len Ebert **160 TR**: Doug Roy **160 BL**: Doug Roy **160 BR**: Doug Roy

Artists represented by Ann Remen-Willis,
Artist Representative and Art Manager:
Len Ebert
Susan Jaekel
Renate Lohmann
Jane McCreary
Carol Newsome
Doug Roy
Rosiland Solomon
Siri Weber Feeney